WE ARE PRESENTLY SEEKING THE SUPPORT OF SOCIETY IN HOPES of being once again accepted. . . . We are all human and make mistakes from time to time. But we all can be productive and industrious. . . . We are asking you, the concerned people of society . . . to come and see for yourself what we are trying to do and, if it's possible, for you to look into the kindness of your hearts to help us by sharing your personal experiences with us. We ask that you help us to grow as you have grown and know as you do that we can and will be accepted once again.

Prison Inmate
Hagerstown, MD

From Cell to Society

**Judith M. Schloegel
and
Robert L. Kinast**

WILLIAM B. EERDMANS PUBLISHING COMPANY
GRAND RAPIDS, MICHIGAN

Copyright © 1988 by Wm. B. Eerdmans Publishing Co.
255 Jefferson Ave. S.E., Grand Rapids, Mich. 49503

Library of Congress Cataloging-in-Publication Data

Schloegel, Judith M.
   From cell to society / Judith M. Schloegel and Robert L. Kinast
     p.   cm.
   ISBN 0-8028-0358-X
   1. Ex-convicts—Employment—United States. 2. Rehabilitation of
criminals—United States. 3. Liberation of Ex-Offenders through
Employment Opportunities (Program) 4. Church work with criminals—
United States.
   I. Kinast, Robert L. II. Title.
HV9304.S337 1988
364.8—dc19
                                                          88-7127
                                                         CIP

Contents

Acknowledgments

This book is lovingly dedicated to Frank and Jerry Schloegel, whose lifetime of service and generosity is the unwritten, inspiring story behind the text which follows.

Special thanks to Mr. William H. G. FitzGerald, whose generous financial support helped make this book possible; to Mrs. Tamlyn Rayle, whose adept typing and editing made the manuscript ready for publication; and to Mr. William B. Eerdmans, Jr., whose interest in this project helped find a way to turn it into a book.

Introduction

Crime concerns everyone. It is a major item on the social agenda in the United States. Ordinarily crime is dealt with by reaffirming the principles of law and order. These principles often result in excessive jail confinement prior to trial, mandatory sentencing, parole restrictions, and increased prison construction.

Crime *is* a major problem in the U.S. and there are no easy solutions to it. But there are alternative approaches and untapped resources. When men or women are released from prison, the foremost challenge they face in making the transition from the cell to society is to find employment. At this crucial stage in their transition, they receive very little assistance from the criminal justice system or from society at large. And yet, employment could be one of the greatest deterrents to subsequent crime.

This book is the story of one program which took an alternative approach and used, quite successfully, the untapped resource of employment to help meet the crime problem. The program is called Liberation of Ex-Offenders Through Employment Opportunities, or LEEO. The LEEO story is presented by Dr. Judith Schloegel, who developed and directed LEEO from 1977 to 1984, and by Dr. Robert L. Kinast, who was a consultant and board member during that period. It is a story that is special in many ways.

It is special first of all because of the women and men whose lives it embraces. These are primarily ex-offenders. Contrary to popular stereotype, the ex-offenders in the LEEO story manifested a deep sense of self-worth and human dignity. They possessed inner resources which they drew upon in the face of adversity to generate hope, courage, and perseverance. They had gifts which enabled LEEO to work *with* them more than for them.

In addition to the ex-offenders, the LEEO story includes employers, the LEEO staff, government officials, church members, family, and friends. In telling their stories, the authors have altered the actual names to preserve confidentiality. But all references and all events are based on what actually happened and complete documentation is available.

This story is special also because it represents a unique integration of religious and secular values, systems, resources, and experiences. From the beginning, LEEO was an explicitly Christian service—but it did not wish to be exclusively Christian. It had to make adaptations, be innovative, take risks, and preserve its identity. Thus LEEO is the story of a Christian ministry which was worked out in the demanding market-place of business, government, and society.

Finally, this story is special because it offers a rich experience from which much learning can be derived. This learning concerns, first of all, the meaning of liberation in both a societal and Christian sense. But it is a learning that includes other values and other forms of social concern. Indeed the primary reason for telling the LEEO story is to present its learning about liberation and about a more general caring for society.

The format for doing so is as follows. Chapter one tells the story of LEEO factually. It is a chronology of what happened between October 1, 1977 and May 1, 1984.

Chapters two through five tell the stories of four LEEO participants. In some respects these stories typify the hundreds of others that could have been told. In other respects each one is unique and has a distinctive contribution to make in expressing what liberation meant.

Chapters six and seven retell the story of LEEO more in terms of caring for society than liberation. Accordingly, two major poles of care are the basis for the presentation: societal environment and caring persons. Chapter six discusses five characteristics of the societal environment in which LEEO functioned and chapter seven discusses five characteristics of the persons who enabled LEEO to function within that environment. These ten characteristics are presented with illustrations from the LEEO experience and in reference, once again, to the Christian Scriptures. They represent transferable and generalizable lessons from LEEO.

The final chapter returns to the prison and shares from a sampling of letters the experience of inmates who still wait, usually with nothing else to do, until they are released and begin the imposing task of returning to society. Several suggestions are offered about what can be done to make the transition from the cell to society more positive and productive.

An epilogue carries the LEEO story in a new direction, toward an innovative use of the private sector within the prison setting. This epilogue describes Judith's work since she left LEEO and brings her efforts up to date.

LEEO's story is part of a complex, dynamic process. It is a creative, challenging, and risky process. LEEO tried to remain firmly rooted in the sources of Christian faith while constantly looking for innovative ways to enact those sources in a liberating and caring way. How LEEO sought to do this is what the following chapters seek to present.

PART ONE

From the Cell to Society

THE STORY OF LEEO is a chronicle of attempts to turn liberation from an ideal into a reality. In doing so, the LEEO program had to free itself from unnecessary restrictions and claim the freedom to use new language, test new methods, form new alliances, and learn from new experiences. Liberation was part of the program's name but it also characterized the program's efforts. This chapter is a chronology of LEEO's first seven years told from the point of view of its first director, Dr. Judith Schloegel. It sets the stage for everything else which follows.

CHAPTER ONE

The LEEO Story

GETTING INVOLVED

THE INVITATION SEEMED SIMPLE ENOUGH: to participate in several consultative visits to the Federal Reformatory for Women located in Alderson, West Virginia. These visits were organized by the Institute of Women Today, founded to "search for the religious and historical roots of women's liberation."

As a member of the Institute, I was invited to join a team composed of lawyers, psychologists, historians, and educators to bring a variety of services to the women in Alderson. Such service to women in prisons is one of the Institute's several programs. In 1976 and 1977 several "prison weekends" were conducted during which members of the Institute spent weekends in the Alderson prison offering individual and group sessions to the women.

As I thought about going to visit a prison, I began to feel apprehension and reluctance. I had no previous experience with the prison system, criminals, or ex-offenders. Besides, I doubted if I had anything to offer prison inmates and in all honesty feared for my personal safety while inside the prison. But I went anyway.

Upon arriving at Alderson, my concerns vanished quickly. In fact the experience of being with those residents became a turning point in my life. Their openness and friendliness endeared them to me immediately, and each story of their involvement with the criminal justice system drew me deeper into their struggle.

I began to realize the horrible injustice of incarcerating these women, many of whom had been convicted of nonviolent crimes and had received far more severe sentences than their male co-defendants. One such case involved Sheila, a young mother from Atlanta where I was living at the time. Sheila had been with her brother during his sale of narcotics to an undercover government agent. Her charge as an accomplice in the sale was a first offense and she had a young daughter to care for. But these facts had little bearing on the lengthy term of imprisonment she received. I found that I was able to offer Sheila and her family some assistance through my contacts in Atlanta. This expedited Sheila's early release from Alderson and assured her of an excellent employment opportunity at a TV station in Atlanta.

Through the entire ordeal it was Sheila's deep faith which proved to be her greatest source of hope. My encounter with her as well as many others in Alderson began to turn the meaning of service inside out for me. Their witness of faith struggle had truly become a source of faith for me.

During subsequent visits, I experienced a growing desire to direct my service to the area of prison work. In February 1977, Dorothy Day, founder of the Catholic Worker Movement, joined the team for a visit to Alderson. The evenings I spent with Dorothy during that weekend reinforced the direction I was feeling.

Dorothy's commitment to service was characterized by a sense of urgency to be with the poor and the outcast and by an inner freedom to make whatever changes are necessary in order to respond fully to all that the Lord invites us to become. (It had become clear to me that I was to make a significant change in service.) My awareness of the struggle of those imprisoned women was becoming my strength as I began a transition from one form of service to another, one which was to become the most meaningful of my life.

In attempting to discern the next step toward service to the imprisoned, I sought the advice of one of the members of the administrative team at Alderson. She suggested that I begin working as a volunteer within a prison setting in Atlanta. She also encouraged me to move to Washington, D.C., where I might more effectively inquire into prison administration opportunities within the Federal Bureau of Prisons.

At her suggestion I began working as a volunteer counselor for women in the Atlanta City Prison Farm. Residents were convicted of misdemeanors, usually disorderly conduct and alcohol abuse. Most of them were over fifty years of age and had few if any sources of support, personally or in the Atlanta community. The experience of working with these women and members of their families only reinforced my convictions about prison service.

I was drawn to them through love because of their tenacity in the midst of human struggle and pain. They wanted to believe in themselves; they wished they could believe in others; and they desperately believed in their God. I found myself empowered through the witness of their hoping and believing. I longed to help liberate those caught in systems of discrimination and indifference.

In July 1977 I moved to the Washington, D.C., area and began scheduling interviews with representatives from the Federal Bureau of Prisons, as well as from local community-based corrections agencies. My postdoctoral professional experience both in administration and in work with emotionally disturbed youth and adults qualified me for positions of leadership in the field of corrections.

Early in September I was informed of an effort initiated by the American Lutheran Church to begin a job placement program for women and men who had been released from prison after completing sentences for felony convictions. Little did I know at that moment that the Spirit was on the move.

LINKING WITH LEEO

On September 1, 1976, representatives from Lutheran agencies and Lutheran congregations in the metropolitan Washington area had submitted a proposal to the American Lutheran Church. Their project was entitled Lutherans Involved in Ex-Offender Employment Opportunities. The stated goal was "to provide increased and improved job opportunities for ex-offenders in the Washington, D.C., metropolitan area."

This project would "directly result in the job placement of at least two ex-offenders per week (average) within six months of the start of the project." Submitting such a proposal to the American Lutheran Church was very appropriate. The Lutheran United Mission Appeal Funding Category VII states that "funding will be used for congregation-related projects in support of self-development among groups of persons who have lacked opportunity, are discriminated against and/or are oppressed."

Four congregations were prepared to assume the responsibility for implementing and monitoring a job placement service for ex-offenders. They are St. Matthew Lutheran Church, Washington, D.C.; Lord of Life Lutheran Church, Fairfax, Virginia; Grace Lutheran Church, Bowie, Maryland; and Bethlehem Lutheran Church, Fairfax, Virginia. The congregations were ready to make a financial commitment to the project, contingent upon initiating money from the American Lutheran Church/United Mission Appeal Office.

The American Lutheran Church responded affirmatively to the proposal, agreeing to award $40,000 over a two-year period. Each of the four congregations would commit $3,000 for the same period. With the total of $52,000 assured, representatives from the four congregations formed a Board of Directors and began the task of identifying a director for the project.

According to the job description, they were "searching for an individual to work full-time in contacting D.C. area employers for the purpose of making jobs directly available to ex-offenders." This project was intended to be a sign of Christian ministry. "In a very real sense the individual to be employed for the purposes of this project will be a missionary. . . . It will be necessary for this person to possess two qualities. First, she/he will need to be an individual with a very strong Christian commitment; secondly, she/he must be someone who understands and relates to the employer's world."

I was intrigued when I first heard of the project from a friend who was a Lutheran deaconess. As my friend outlined the goals of the project and shared the frustration of the board in not having been able to identify a director, my interest piqued. Thirty-seven individuals had been interviewed and a meeting had been scheduled in a few days to identify a final candidate. I felt a strong urge to appear before the board in order to see firsthand what this project was all about. My friend eagerly invited me.

Little did I know as I walked into the silent, empty church hall of First Trinity Lutheran Church the night of September 15, 1977, that by September 15, 1984, that same church hall would be the location for the most supportive, liberating, and successful job placement service for ex-offenders that Washington had ever known. During the interview, board members impressed me with their obvious commitment to help ex-offenders become self-reliant, contributing members of society through gainful employment opportunities. These concerned Christians had clearly integrated the proposed employment project with their own faith in the Lord's call to be people of mission. As a Roman Catholic sister, my own commitment to Christian ministry resonated with theirs. In addition, I responded satisfactorily to their questions about how I would effectively engage prospective employers in the difficult task of placing women and men, convicted of serious crimes, in the job market.

I left the meeting feeling good about the discussion and I felt even better the following morning when the phone rang with the news, "Can you meet us on September 18 to sign a contract for the position of director?"

"Yes, oh yes!"

LEEO UNDER LUTHERAN SPONSORSHIP

(October 1, 1977–September 30, 1979)

LEEO was to be in operation by October 1, 1977. As the director and only staff member of the program, I set up my office on the second floor of an old house adjacent to First Trinity Lutheran Church. The facility belonged to the church and housed a community-based organization called Community Family Life Services which provided food, clothing, counseling, and related services to those in need—many of whom were ex-offenders. Their service, sponsored and operated by First Trinity as well as other local Lutheran agencies and congregations, offered valuable support and cooperation during four important phases of program development.

Phase 1: The Foundation

(October–November 1977)

The first task was to lay the foundation for LEEO. Specific objectives for phase 1 included (1) contacting representatives of established, community-based corrections agencies to acquaint them with LEEO and to establish linkages for the referral of those on probation and parole; (2) identifying available resources in the metropolitan D.C. area which could help meet job-related needs (transportation, work clothes, tools) of LEEO participants; (3) listing potential sources of employment in the metropolitan D.C. area; (4) developing an action plan by which a person released from prison would make an effective transition to the world of work; (5) addressing Lutheran church groups in order to keep them informed about the program they were helping to fund as well as to solicit their assistance with the job placement of program participants.

Laying the foundation presented a double challenge. In preparing materials for presentations to community representatives and prospective employers, I was ready to debate the question of ex-offender employment from a practical, moral, juridical, or economic point of view. I had identified specific incentives for employers who would hire ex-offenders through LEEO. I felt prepared. But then I discovered a second challenge.

While most people found such a project as LEEO interesting, few were willing to take it seriously. They were skeptical that such a program would ever succeed. A well-known expert in the field of corrections from a local university even remarked, "You have three strikes against you. You're a woman; you're white; and you're religious."

It became clear that the issue of credibility was foundational to the success of LEEO. Without having placed a single ex-offender in a job, it was impossible for me to point to results. So I turned to endorsements. Mrs. Coretta Scott King responded with the first of several significant expressions of support from people who would get the attention of those I contacted. Her letter and the inspiration of Dr. King's work continually grounded LEEO's efforts. She said in part:

> I am especially gratified by the sense of social responsibility and practical commitment being evidenced by the Lutheran Churches who are sponsoring and funding the program. As you know, my husband repeatedly challenged the Christian Churches to courageously accept and to live out the fullness of their divine mission. . . . As we continue our efforts to achieve a full employment economy for our nation, we will be especially mindful of your efforts and of the employment needs of the men and women you will be serving. . . . My commendation, also, to all of the employers who will be working with you in this most worthy endeavor. . . . My warm greetings and every encouragement to our brothers and sisters whom you will be serving. Their 'new day' is keeping the 'dream' alive.

By November 30, 1977, the foundation had been laid. A sufficient number of contacts had been made. The stage was set. It was time to build on the foundation and welcome the women and men for whom LEEO had been designed.

Phase 2: The Structure

(December 1977–February 1978)

The main goal in phase 2 was to set up the structure which would enable LEEO to work effectively. Specific objectives included (1) developing a referral procedure by which women and men who were on probation or parole would apply for admittance into LEEO; (2) screening applicants who were eligible for LEEO services; (3) establishing meaningful relationships with those who were admitted into LEEO in order to prepare them for employment, secure resources for their job-related needs, and identify an appropriate job for them; (4) visiting numerous employers in order to identify those who would be willing to hire an ex-offender after February 1.

In order to set up an appropriate structure, I had to become very familiar with the conditions and backgrounds which characterized most of the applicants. During these two months I learned that they were all convicted of a felony and many of them had a history of criminal behavior. Their charges included burglary, kidnapping, aggravated assault, rape, forgery, drug possession or sales, embezzlement, murder, and grand larceny.

Second, they were either on probation or parole. Only occasionally had an applicant completed the full sentence while incarcerated.

Third, they had an inferior educational level. Even though the average age of the applicants was between 29 and 35, the average grade of school completed was only tenth.

Fourth, they were responsible for dependents. Sixty-three percent of the applicants had children for whom they were responsible.

Fifth, they had inadequate work experience in the past. Most applicants had less than six consecutive months of work experience prior to being admitted into LEEO.

Sixth, they had poverty-level income. Most applicants had grown up and were currently living in substandard housing conditions.

Finally, they were unprepared for the work environment. Most were not ready to perform satisfactorily in a job interview. In addition, they lacked the skills for adequate functioning and adjustment in the work environment.

Of particular concern to me were the female applicants. I had been sensitized to the experience of women in prison through my work at Alderson. Women who had experienced the dehumanization of imprisonment required extensive supportive services. For those who had been incarcerated, the scars of having been separated from their children healed slowly. Often, upon release from the institution, women would find that their children had been moved from family to family and their relationship with the children suffered. The emotional and psychological effects of having experienced the criminal justice system appeared to break down the self-image and self-confidence of women more than of men. At times, they seemed marked by a self-fulfilling prophecy: "See, I told I you I wouldn't get the job." "I knew the employer would not hire me." "I know I'll never make it."

As the number of women and men applicants increased gradually over this two-month period, I grew in my understanding and appreciation of each participant. I was edified by their openness, grateful for their trust, strengthened by their sense of hope, and challenged by their willingness to struggle. In truth, the women and men of LEEO were to become the single most significant source of encouragement to me over the years. If they were willing to strive for employment opportunities in the midst of discrimination and calculated exclusion, how could I do anything less than whatever it would take to find them a job—and even more, to help them keep it.

Phase 3: Implementation

(February–June 1978)

The purpose of setting up the structure was to implement the program. Specific objectives of the implementation phase included (1) placing LEEO participants in suitable employment opportunities; (2) following up those women and men who had been placed in jobs, as well as maintaining regular contacts with their employers; (3) continuing communication efforts to heighten the visibility and credibility of LEEO in the D.C. area.

LEEO was now in full operation. By June 1978, eighty-eight persons had applied to LEEO. I was making four to six job placements a month. My efforts to secure jobs from prospective employers were enhanced by the number of companies who were beginning to hire through LEEO. This became a valuable strategy in approaching new companies.

I would always try to make an appointment with the president of a corporation. After carefully outlining the purpose and structure of LEEO, I would suggest reasons and incentives for the corporation to hire a LEEO participant. However, nothing seemed more relevant than citing the other corporations who had experienced success in working with LEEO. At this point, the individual with whom I was meeting would usually express interest in and commendation of the work of LEEO. "The next step would be for you to meet with the Director of the Personnel Division . . . and please indicate that I asked you to call for an appointment."

That was what I was waiting for. When I contacted the personnel division, my reference to the corporation's president was the ticket in the door. Not knowing the context of the relationship but wanting, of course, to appear cooperative, the personnel manager would, in most cases, be very responsive to the possibility of hiring a LEEO participant. Even though this meant starting all over again explaining the purpose of LEEO and incentives for hiring through LEEO, it was always worth it.

Of course, getting the initial appointment with a company president usually came only after many phone calls, several contacts, and the patient waiting for "I'll-get-back-to-you." Sometimes, however, there were commitments which came as a surprise (and always, it seemed, when I was beginning to wonder if it was all worth it).

One such surprise occurred after I had addressed a Lutheran congregation during one of their Sunday worship services. As I was leaving the church, a man approached and handed me a slip of paper on which he had written his name and phone number. He said, "Call me at the office tomorrow." When I dialed the number the following morning, I was greeted with the name of one of the most prestigious universities in the metropolitan area. The individual, it turned out, was a vice president of the university. He referred me to their Director of Personnel. This contact would lead to twenty-nine placements at that university over a two-year period.

The range of employers grew as LEEO implemented its program: two hospitals, three service agencies, three universities, a passport company, an automotive glass repair company, a library, a landscaping company, a carpentry firm, a major telephone company, a management firm, an electronics corporation, the National Weather Bureau Service, a private school, a floor service company, and a printing firm. The lowest salary was $3.50 an hour and the highest was $5.33 an hour. The recidivism rate (or conviction for a new crime) of those who had been placed in jobs through LEEO remained less than 5 percent.

To enhance LEEO's credibility was a constant task. Endorsements and successful job placements were very helpful and led to a third source, the public media. Early in February 1978 I had called Mr. William Raspberry, one of the editorial writers for the *Washington Post*. I discussed with him the purpose of LEEO and expressed my hope that he would write an editorial describing LEEO's efforts. Being the wise and practical person he is, Mr. Raspberry suggested that I call him back when LEEO participants had indeed been hired. He preferred covering a story of what *was* happening rather than a story of what was *going* to happen. After I had secured the seventeenth job placement, I called him. He agreed to see me. In June 1978 the *Washington Post* printed his editorial entitled, "Wanted: Employers for Ex-Offenders."

The value of this article in furthering LEEO's visibility and credibility can never be fully appreciated. It significantly strengthened subsequent contacts with prospective employers and funding sources. The response of Mr. Raspberry to my request was even more meaningful to me for personal reasons. In our initial discussion Mr. Raspberry had not been impressed simply with the initiation of another jobs program. Rather, he seemed to be drawn to LEEO's story precisely because of the commitment to and quality of service for human beings. His own sense of justice and concern for others prompted the editorial.

I began to recognize this same type of response from employers, representatives from community organizations, and government personnel. Regardless of their diversity, people felt drawn to contribute to the effort of providing opportunities for those who were otherwise labeled "outcasts." It was time to take stock. In June 1978 the LEEO board spent a full day with me reviewing the accomplishments and planning for the future. I had only one request for discussion at the meeting, a request I felt deeply about.

Phase 4: Expansion

(July 1978–September 1979)

After the initial success of the LEEO program, it was time to start thinking about expansion. Specific objectives in phase 4 included (1) developing LEEO's method of screening, job placement, and follow-up of program participants; (2) expanding the LEEO staff; (3) securing funds for the program upon the completion of the two-year financial commitment of the Lutheran church.

At the June 1978 meeting with the LEEO board, everyone took delight in the accomplishments of LEEO since its beginning on October 1, 1977. However, I expressed my concern at the growing pressure to meet program objectives and offer quality service to program participants. I requested additional staff to meet this need and the board readily approved. That decision sparked an expansion over the next five years that would culminate in a comprehensive network of services for ex-offenders provided by a staff of professionally qualified, committed individuals. Such expansion would also demand intense fundraising efforts and the assistance of hundreds of individuals.

In July 1978 two persons joined the LEEO staff. Both were ex-offenders who brought to LEEO's efforts their own life experience, competence, and sense of commitment. With their assistance, program participants benefited from improved job readiness and job-related services and a more intensive period of follow-up supervision once they were employed. The number of job placements continued to grow and by September it was time to celebrate.

On the evening of September 24, two hundred people gathered for an Awards Night. The celebration was intended to congratulate program participants who had successfully secured a job and to recognize those employers who had been willing to give the ex-offenders a chance through employment. The service was ecumenical and included a Roman Catholic priest, a Lutheran pastor, an Islamic imam, and a Baptist minister. Thirty-four ex-offenders were awarded certificates of commendation and each of their employers was recognized for cooperation in hiring. Special appreciation was extended to members of the Lutheran church, to the many metropolitan agencies who had provided supportive services, and to the staff and board of LEEO.

The final benediction summarized the experience.

O God, you desire that each of us should live a full, happy life in this world. You are always ready to help us even when we make mistakes. You never abandon us or give up hope for us. And you call us to help and support one another. Bless us who have gathered here tonight. We strive to live as the people you would have us be—forgiving, caring, generous, and loving. Bless those who have made this program possible, who have worked so hard to bring it from an idea to a reality. Bless those who have offered jobs, who have shown support and interest, who have volunteered to be of service. Bless the clients who have taken advantage of this chance, who have put their trust in others, who have shown their determination and sincerity. Finally, bless those who are still afraid, still victims of prejudice, still unconcerned about the persons who need help. Bless them with your spirit of change, of openness, of responsiveness. And help us all to grow more deeply in your love and more fully in your life as we share this night together in your name. Amen.

The expansion of services and staff required more operating space. First Trinity Lutheran Church had housed the program from its inception. Now the generosity of First Trinity was demonstrated once again. Through the volunteer efforts of congregation members and with the support of the LEEO board, additional office space was provided in the church hall and in January 1979 LEEO had a new home.

The appropriateness of expanding the staff and increasing office space was reflected in the ongoing achievements of LEEO. One hundred fifty ex-offenders had applied for admission; 125 prison inmates from federal and state institutions throughout the country had contacted LEEO for assistance; 78 persons had been admitted into

LEEO; 63 jobs or training opportunities had been secured; 29 businesses had hired LEEO participants.

By now, examples of upward mobility for those who had been employed through LEEO were beginning to surface. One female participant who had been hired by a local university received a salary increase of $1,000. Another participant working in a boiler room had been promoted to an apprentice engineer.

Some of the placements had disappointing outcomes, however. Several persons lost their jobs after having been employed for one to three months. A second (and in some cases a third) placement seemed necessary in order for them to adjust fully to the expectations of the work environment. Occasionally, the personal goals and expectations of those employed were unrealistic. As a result, retention rates for on-the-job performance were reduced. Some were unable to postpone gratification or to "start from the bottom and work their way up." This led to job and program terminations. For others, it was difficult to work for $3.50 an hour when they could hustle on the streets and make $350.00 in a very short period.

All these facts called for increased response from LEEO. By February 1979 the LEEO staff included a communication specialist, a coordinator of program services, and a coordinator of supportive services. The actual assistance was provided by other agencies in the areas of career assessment and related counseling, emergency supportive services, and special guidance for participants who were veterans. Needless to say, this array of services significantly enhanced the continuous efforts to place the women and men of LEEO in suitable jobs.

But there was concern about finding additional sources of funding to keep the expanded program going. By September 30, 1979, the Lutheran church's two-year grant would be depleted. There was no question that LEEO should continue; the only question was, with what sources of funding could it continue?

By April 1979, the board and I knew the gravity of the situation. We had solicited funding assistance from over a thousand area businesses, local foundations, and national funding sources. The positive results of these efforts were insufficient. It was clear that remaining funds would have to be restricted and program services severely limited. Contracts for salaried staff were terminated on April 1, 1979. In the next months, I endeavored to conduct limited job development and follow-up support for those who had been placed in jobs through LEEO. During this period, three faithful, hard-working volunteers assisted in keeping the program in operation while members of the board and I attempted to find new sources of funding.

With the depletion of Lutheran funding on September 30, the board and I concurred that the title of the program, Lutherans Involved in Ex-Offender Employment Opportunities, would no longer be appropriate. It was at the suggestion of the board's president, who had worked tirelessly to secure ongoing funding for the program, that the new name of the program, effective October 1, 1979, would be Liberation of Ex-Offenders through Employment Opportunities.

And liberate they would!

LEEO IN A PERIOD OF TRANSITION

(October 1, 1979–April 30, 1980)

Under Lutheran sponsorship, LEEO had been a productive and successful ministry. The statistics speak for themselves. Three hundred ex-offenders had applied for admittance into LEEO by phone or visits to the office. An additonal 206 inmates had forwarded letters to LEEO for job assistance upon release and fifty-two agencies or individuals had referred ex-offenders to LEEO. One hundred thirty-three ex-offenders had been admitted into the program and had received some level of service.

One hundred twenty-two jobs or training opportunities had been secured for LEEO participants. Forty-six metropolitan area businesses had hired participants through LEEO and ninety-four companies had expressed a willingness to hire through LEEO at a future time.

Seventy-five referrals to community service organizations had been made through LEEO to help meet some of the basic human needs of participants. Twenty-six participants had been certified for the Targeted Jobs Tax Credit which provided a tax credit to the employers who had hired them. Five participants employed through LEEO had been bonded through the Federal Bonding Program. Two hundred forty individuals had expressed an interest in and support of LEEO by offering their volunteer assistance or expressing a willingness to be of help at a future time.

Despite sixty financial commitments made by individuals, churches, community organizations, or businesses, the funding needs of LEEO were acute. So for the remainder of 1979, I concentrated primarily on raising the necessary funds to keep LEEO going. As a result,

my efforts to provide screening, job readiness, job placement, and follow-up were significantly reduced. This reduction was not due solely
to the time demanded for fundraising but was also in large part the result of a tragic occurrence in the life of one of the participants.

George Martin had been admitted into LEEO on June 21, 1978. He
was forty-four years old, married, and the father of three children. He
had completed twelve grades of school and earned a high school degree
while serving time in prison. His past convictions included theft of
government property, robbery, automobile theft, and carrying an unli-
censed weapon. As in the case of many applicants who had served their
sentence and had grown more mature, George was highly motivated to
turn his life around and secure a meaningful job. He longed to become
a self-reliant, contributing member of his family and of society.

During the pre-employment period with LEEO, George gladly volunteered his assistance to the program. He could be called upon at any
time for help with office mailings in fundraising attempts. George was
willing to be interviewed on local TV for a program highlighting LEEO.
His hobby was photography and whenever photographs were needed
for publicity on LEEO, George not only took all the pictures, but he had
them developed at no cost to the program.

On September 14, 1978, George was hired by the housekeeping
department of a local hospital. His position was service worker and his
salary was $4.00 an hour. Because of his employment through LEEO
and the significant efforts he had made toward rehabilitation, George
was paroled by the District of Columbia Parole Board on December 7,
1978. He left the halfway house that morning and went to a florist to
buy me a dozen roses. As he walked into my office, I recognized in him
the liberated spirit which I often experienced with the participants of
LEEO. His potential for giving, trusting, and respecting others had become actualized.

George maintained his job with a high level of performance until
May 1979. Then he began to encounter difficulties on the job site. Because follow-up services for those employed had been significantly reduced, I was not in regular contact with George or with his employer.
On May 11, 1979, George was terminated from his job for "insubordi-
nation."

Having lost his job and the steady income he had become dependent on over the previous eight months, George began to withdraw from
his family and friends. He turned to gambling and on the night of June
1, he forfeited his prized camera in a poker game. In desperation he

went to his home for a knife and returned, determined to get his camera back by force. The man who had his camera also had a gun and warned George not to come any closer or he would shoot him. George's last words were, "Go ahead and shoot me." As he charged the man, George was shot and killed.

The impact of that incident affected me deeply. I became aware of LEEO's serious responsibility to provide proper and complete services for its participants. I sensed the inherent danger of exploiting program members. It was possible to meet certain program objectives regarding job placement but to neglect other, real needs of those placed in jobs. I was convinced that if LEEO had provided George and his employer consistent support for one year, George would not have been killed. I was determined to develop a more holistic approach to the job placement process before additional women and men would be admitted into LEEO. The standards of the medical profession offered an apt comparison. No hospital would admit patients, perform necessary surgery, and then leave the patients to care for themselves. If LEEO were to continue, its own integrity demanded a more comprehensive approach to the services it provided, and that meant money.

The many letters of request and funding proposals submitted in 1979 began to bear fruit in 1980. Individuals, foundations, businesses, and churches responded, but the funding required to hire professional staff for the needed delivery of services once again far exceeded the amount raised from individual sources. It was clear that a major source of funding would have to be identified.

In the meantime, from December 1979 through March 1980, I served as a consultant to the National Alliance of Business. This allowed me to maintain my own salary as well as keep the LEEO office open. As consultant I processed all requests from ex-offenders who contacted the Washington office of the National Alliance of Business for assistance. With the help of two volunteers, I kept the LEEO office open, responding to calls, letters, and office visits from ex-offenders. Services to participants were put on hold, with the exception of limited follow-up for those who had been employed through LEEO. All available time was given to securing a large grant.

As it turned out, my association with the National Alliance of Business proved to be most efficacious. In the spring of 1980 a new community organization, the Washington, D.C., Private Industry Council (PIC), was developed under the auspices of the National Department of

Labor and in cooperation with the D.C. Department of Employment Services.

The PIC was composed of representatives from business, labor, government, and community-based organizations. Members were appointed to the PIC by the mayor of Washington. Among the PIC's primary functions was to solicit proposals from local agencies and organizations to offer employment and training services to disadvantaged, underemployed D.C. residents. Funding grants from the Department of Labor were to be awarded by the PIC for those proposals which outlined appropriate action plans and a system for determining measurable results. There was a close linkage between the PIC and the National Alliance of Business. My association with the latter generated an awareness of and interest in LEEO among the PIC members.

With the assistance of the president of the LEEO board and the competent, volunteer service of his wife, I submitted a proposal to the PIC in March 1980. This proposal, entitled Ex-Offender Job Placement (EJP), had two major components: first, an extensive lobby of community representatives who would offer their endorsement of LEEO in the form of a letter addressed to the PIC, and second, a comprehensive organization of services in the areas of employment and training which would be provided through LEEO for ex-offenders.

There was an overwhelming response to the request for endorsement. The Washington, D.C., community clearly recognized the contribution of LEEO over the previous two years and was eager to see the program continue.

The proposal outlined a comprehensive approach for providing ex-offenders with quality job placement services. The services were organized within units in the following sequence.

Unit 1: *Referral.* All ex-offenders would be D.C. residents, convicted of a felony, and of poverty income as determined by the D.C. Department of Employment Services. Women and men would be initially screened and referred to LEEO by four local corrections agencies to be known as LEEO Satellites. They were the D.C. Department of Corrections, the Federal Probation/District Court Office, the D.C. Superior Court, and the Bureau of Rehabilitation.

Unit 2: *Screening.* A LEEO staff member would interview and determine the eligibility of each applicant according to the following criteria: (1) the applicant had no current drug, alcohol, or behavioral problem; (2) the applicant was able to work full time, five days a week; (3) the applicant was highly motivated to find and keep a job.

Unit 3: *Job Readiness*. A LEEO staff member would conduct activities designed to prepare an underemployed felon for the world of work. Participants' attendance, daily contact with the program, attitudes, and aptitude for employment would be monitored closely by the LEEO staff.

Unit 4: *Job Development and Placement*. Two job developers on the LEEO staff would contact area businesses by phone, mailings, and office visits to secure job placements for LEEO participants. An organized, sequential plan for job interviews would ideally result in an appropriate match between the program participants and a suitable job.

Unit 5: *Follow-up Supervision and Supportive Services*. A staff member would conduct a one-year follow-up beginning immediately after job placement. This follow-up would include regular phone contacts and job site visits with both the program participants and the employer. In addition, job-related needs (e.g., transportation assistance, uniforms) would be requested from local community service organizations and monitored by another LEEO staff member.

Unit 6: *Bookkeeping and Clerical Assistance*. The staff would include a part-time bookkeeper, who had already been volunteering her assistance in this capacity over the past year, and a clerical assistant who would work full time.

The plan was complete; community support was apparent; ex-offenders were hopeful. Then, late in April 1980 word came. Get on with your liberation; the proposal was funded. It was a new day for LEEO.

LEEO UNDER PUBLIC AND PRIVATE FUNDING

(May 1, 1980–May 1, 1984)

During this period of funding by the Private Industry Council, there had been four significant factors in the LEEO story: on-going program development, the impact of the media on LEEO's efforts, heightened visibility of the program through staff and program activities, and my resignation as the executive director of LEEO.

On-going Program Development

The first government grant awarded to LEEO by the PIC covered operating expenses from May 1, 1980 through September 30, 1980. It was assumed that the PIC would renew and increase this grant for the subsequent fiscal year, October 1, 1980 through September 30, 1981. Such was the case, but future funding was contingent on the success of LEEO. The job placement rate of ex-offenders and delivery of services characterized by a high level of quality and accountability led the PIC to award grants to LEEO for each year thereafter.

With the needed funding assured, I was able to hire qualified and committed individuals to fill the staff positions outlined in the proposal. Without question, the success of LEEO over the next four years was a result of the quality services provided to program participants by staff members. Staff positions were filled by different individuals during this four-year period, but each person made valuable contributions to the program. Four staff members who helped implement the original EJP proposal remained on staff through fiscal year 1983–1984. Their leadership brought a dimension of continuity and expansion of service that served as the backbone of the program.

The organizational design of six units was maintained. However, the services provided within these units were improved upon and expanded over the years. This development resulted in additional staff. By 1984 each unit had doubled in staff size and the program was able to admit twice the number of ex-offenders. Services, particularly in the area of job readiness and follow-up supervision and support, were more adequate in meeting the job-related needs of program participants.

By April 1984 the program had grown from the initial staff of one with a two-year budget of $52,000 to a staff of twelve with an annual operating budget of $350,000. The number of job placements had increased from 70 a year to 150 a year. The expansion of job-related services to the women and men of LEEO far surpassed the hopes and intentions of the original goals of LEEO outlined in 1977.

Those who applied for admittance into LEEO found themselves in a supportive, caring environment. They entered a program staffed by persons who offered sensitivity and respect in the initial screening process; effective job readiness activities and pre-employment counseling in their preparation for the world of work; careful and appropriate job development services in their attempts to secure a job; and patient and helpful support in their efforts to maintain employment and refrain from future involvement in criminal behavior.

The support system for the LEEO program was community wide. Upon request, assistance was readily offered by program participant board members, volunteers, community and corrections agencies, government representatives, employers, and my religious community, the Sisters of St. Joseph of Carondolet. From such a solid base, LEEO was able to initiate additional projects to help meet the needs of ex-offenders. These were the LEEO/Lorton Project, the LEEO Job Readiness Unit, and the LEEO/Federal Probation Project.

The LEEO/Lorton Project took the LEEO program into the prison. Funded by a local foundation for six months, the project began on March 12, 1982. Over the six-month period, a LEEO staff member interviewed and screened residents at the Minimum Security Facility in Lorton, Virginia. Once eligibility for LEEO had been determined, residents were admitted into LEEO. These residents were transported by a prison vehicle to the LEEO office site every Tuesday and Thursday. They participated in LEEO job readiness training sessions, attended job interviews scheduled on their behalf, and secured employment under staff supervision. Once employed, these residents were released from prison, assigned to community halfway houses, and subsequently paroled.

The LEEO Job Readiness Unit, also funded by a local foundation, was initiated on April 20, 1982. This unit was intended to expand the existing job readiness services of LEEO. Under this project, a more comprehensive approach to preparing persons for the world of work was developed. It included activities on orientation and assessment, goal setting, job search, work habits, transition from prison to society, and evaluation. This project was subsequently integrated into the LEEO model and funded annually by the PIC.

The LEEO/Federal Probation Project was initiated on June 1, 1983 to permit the referral of drug-free applicants into LEEO through the Federal Probation Aftercare Drug Treatment Program. Under close supervision of both LEEO and Federal Probation staff, those referred were admitted into LEEO for assistance in job readiness, pre-employment counseling, job placement, and a one-year follow-up period.

Impact of the Media

Since its beginning in 1977, LEEO significantly benefited from coverage by the public media. In particular, television and radio interviews brought the story of LEEO to the public's attention. One example of this was a radio interview on December 26, 1980, with the Operations Manager of a large department store on the topic of "Employment Through the LEEO Program." On January 30, 1981, he appeared again, this time on television to discuss the LEEO program from a participating employer's point of view. Because this employer had hired LEEO participants and had experienced a great deal of success in doing so, he was able to demonstrate a high level of commitment and support through his personal testimony.

Most often, these types of programs helped to sensitize the public in general to the issue of ex-offender employment, but television coverage also resulted in financial donations for the program.

During one of the critical funding periods, I contacted a well-known reporter at a local TV station who had previously expressed interest in LEEO. He agreed to highlight LEEO and the program's funding needs during the evening news. On May 1 and May 2, 1979, he appealed to the television audience for financial contributions to help keep the program in operation. Several scenes, filmed earlier in the day, were aired showing program participants engaged in job readiness sessions. These were combined with personal interviews in which participants expressed their sincerity in turning from a life of crime and their willingness to become self-reliant, contributing members of society by means of gainful employment.

Almost a thousand dollars was forwarded to LEEO by viewers who had been positively affected by these broadcasts and who wanted to express their support through their contributions.

Stories about LEEO in newspaper articles by noted columnists as well as notices in trade magazines and community papers both informed the public of LEEO's existence and also solicited sources of employment and financial contributions.

Staff and Program Activities

Of all the methods and techniques developed to increase the credibility and visibility of the LEEO program, no approach met with more success than introducing the LEEO staff. No one was with them for more than five minutes before experiencing their professional expertise and their deep commitment to LEEO and its cause. In addition to individual staff activities conducted on behalf of LEEO, a series of team activities enhanced the image of LEEO both locally and nationally. A few examples follow.

On February 10, 1981, a luncheon for two hundred business leaders in metropolitan Washington was held in a Georgetown restaurant. This event relied on the generosity, support, and cooperation of many persons. The restaurant, owned by a LEEO board member, provided the luncheon at no cost to the program. The event was sponsored by a major corporation in the Washington area and the main address was delivered by the president of the National Alliance of Business. But the success of this luncheon in raising the awareness of local business leaders to the issue of ex-offender employment and the role of LEEO in this endeavor could not have been realized without the cooperation and hard work of the staff in preparing for and executing this event. Their professional presence among the business leaders that afternoon spoke more about the quality and integrity of LEEO than any prepared statement ever could have.

On April 14, 1981, the staff was invited to participate in the Middle Atlantic States Correctional Association Conference. The topic of this conference was Creative Corrections—Sharing What Works. And share they did. The staff described LEEO's services by involving conference participants in simulated sessions. Participants experienced firsthand the screening, job readiness, job development, and follow-up services of LEEO by engaging in individual activities with each staff member. Once again, the professionalism of the staff solidified LEEO's identity as a responsible, successful service in the community.

September 16, 1982 found the staff bound for the Women's Reformatory in Alderson, West Virginia. Little did I know on my last visit there in 1977 that I would be returning in 1982 accompanied by a full staff to offer the residents some specific means for gainful employment upon their release. The staff conducted a two-day, comprehensive workshop in job readiness with the residents. The staff's sensitivity to and support of the imprisoned women was an example of personal commitment to the promise of liberation and a source of hope and courage to the inmates, many of whom would contact LEEO upon their release to the D.C. area.

On November 1, 1983, the LEEO staff participated in an Employers Awareness Breakfast Meeting held at the Greater Washington Board of Trade Office. The meeting was sponsored by the PIC and endorsed by the Washington Correctional Foundation. Once again, the impact of the staff was obvious. While several remarks about the LEEO program had been made and a letter from Senator Arlan Specter commending LEEO's efforts had been read, the real message of the program was conveyed when each staff member introduced him/herself and described the respective services for program participants. This event was to have special meaning for me, however, in my growing deliberation to resign as the executive director of LEEO.

Director's Resignation

Of all the influences on my leadership efforts during the seven years at LEEO, the two most important were my Christian faith and the teachings of Dr. Martin Luther King, Jr. The participants of LEEO brought me face-to-face on a daily basis with life situations in which human pain, struggle, and undying hope were apparent. I had seen the anguish of a rejected people and had been reminded over and over again of those whose lives had been touched by the prophets, by Jesus, and by Dr. King.

My reflection on and study of Dr. King's theology over the years kept me sensitive to and respectful of black persons. The "dream" of Dr. King involved far more than mere racial integration. As he wrote, "true integration means a real share of power and responsibility. . . . We want to be integrated *into* power."

I had been aware that all of the program participants were black, that most of the staff were black, and that I, the director of LEEO, was white. In fact for seven years both the LEEO board and program leadership had been maintained by white persons. The issue of race had not been a conscious factor in either board membership or staff development at LEEO. The priority had always been one's willingness and ability to provide quality service regardless of race or religious preference.

The Employment Awareness Breakfast on November 1, 1983, brought the point home clearly. At the breakfast meeting, the first speakers stood. They represented three local systems of power as well as the administration of LEEO. They were all white. When the persons responsible for the actual delivery of services to LEEO participants were introduced, they stood. Almost all were black.

I realized that the time had come for the leadership of LEEO to be passed to the capable hands of a black person. So, by May 1, 1984, LEEO had new leadership. Both the director of the program and the chairman of the board were black, representing the affirmation of this new leadership.

In seven years, hundreds of women and men had received quality, job-related services. Hundreds more had been encouraged while imprisoned by the very hope and support which LEEO symbolized. And most important, nearly seven hundred jobs had been secured. With the sense of having completed all that I was called to be and offer through my service in this work, I joined my sisters and brothers in a closing song during a farewell celebration. "Reach out and touch somebody's hand; make this world a better place . . ."

Through the power of liberation, LEEO had.

PART TWO

Liberation through LEEO

IN EACH OF THE NEXT FOUR CHAPTERS a specific aspect of liberation in the life of a LEEO participant will be told. These aspects are power, self-perception, systems, and judgment. The basic facts in each story will be presented first. Then the implications of the story for the meaning of liberation will be drawn out. This will be done in two ways.

First, the story will be analyzed or interpreted within a relational view of life. The relational view used for this purpose is derived from the philosophical principles of Alfred North Whitehead and is also known as process philosophy or the philosophy of organism. According to this relational view, life is understood as a process of becoming. The actual process is centered in specific events or occasions. These occasions are the actual experiences which a person has of his or her world. As such, they are uniquely personal creations, drawing upon the many other events which make up one's world but put together in a characteristic way by each person.

This implies that each person's life is a self-creative process, always open to change and characterized by freedom. But it also implies that each person's life is intrinsically related to other events, because other events provide most of the experience which a person draws upon in constructing his or her own life. This interrelationship is a cumulative process, constantly enlarging the total world of experience in which we all live. But it is also a qualitative process, constantly modifying the experiences and feelings which constitute our actual world.

The values and principles of such a relational view of life guided the LEEO program from its inception. These values and principles are widely acknowledged in our American society today although they take many different forms of expression. A relational view of life enabled LEEO many times to communicate its purpose, share its values, and achieve its goals. Consequently, this same view of life will be used to draw out the meaning of liberation in the four cases which follow.

At the same time, a relational view of life does not completely express all the meaning contained in the stories of LEEO. There are other implications for liberation which are part of an explicitly Christian view of life. The Christian perspective was certainly part of LEEO's story and its contribution to the meaning of liberation will also be included. This inclusion is not a mere addendum, although one could read the stories and the relational analyses of them without taking into account the Christian view.

The contribution of a Christian perspective is seen primarily in its own stories. These stories constitute the nucleus of the Christian Scriptures, the New Testament. This material will be used as a kind of parallel process to illustrate how the stories of LEEO reenact the stories of Christian faith. In this way, the fuller (faith) meaning of liberation through LEEO will appear while LEEO's experience will shed some contemporary light on the biblical narratives.

This combination of relational and Christian views of LEEO's story is intended to disclose the meaning which is already contained in the stories themselves. Just as LEEO itself lived in relation to both an inclusive, human experience and an explicit, Christian experience, so the meaning of its story is told from a broad, relational and a specific, biblical view. Together they describe what liberation meant, not on the program's letterhead but in the lives of the program's participants.

CHAPTER TWO

Liberating Power

THE STORY

MIKE LONG WAS FEELING GOOD. He was on parole and had been admitted into the LEEO program on April 4, 1978. At the age of twenty, he had been convicted for conspiracy to rob with a deadly weapon and served three and one-half years in prison.

On April 28, 1978, Mike went on a job interview through the LEEO program and was hired on May 3 as a service worker trainee in a large, Washington, D.C., hospital. His salary was $3.75 an hour. He was subsequently promoted to service worker at $3.85 an hour; then his salary was raised to $4.15 an hour.

Mike had understood the gravity of his crime and was remorseful. His efforts toward rehabilitation had been exemplary. He demonstrated responsible and cooperative behavior while under parole supervision and maintained an excellent employment history in his job at the hospital.

Then, on the evening of November 11, 1978, Mike and his wife, Carla, went to a shopping mall to purchase an umbrella. Mike looked around in a large department store while Carla went to a mailbox at the end of the mall to mail a letter. Mike picked out an umbrella he liked but wanted to show it to Carla before making the purchase. From the door of the store, he saw her coming through the mall. He stepped out of the store with the umbrella in his hand and the sales ticket hanging from it. A security guard who had been watching Mike arrested him immediately and charged him with theft. Mike was handcuffed and transported to a county jail. One week later his family was finally able to post the required bond. Mike was released and ordered to appear at a hearing. A trial was later scheduled for May 4, 1979. Having informed his supervisor at the hospital of the situation when he was arrested, Mike was able to return to his job.

On April 19, I received a summons to appear before the circuit court for Prince Georges County in Upper Marlboro, Maryland, to testify in Mike's defense. The prosecution apparently was attempting to build its case on the fact that Mike had been convicted in the past for "conspiracy to rob." This was to suggest that he was guilty in the present situation. So Mike needed character witnesses.

He requested that his supervisor from the hospital attend the trial in his defense. Mike's work supervisor was more than happy to do so. In fact, he took a day off from work, without pay, in order to be present. He was prepared to offer a character reference on behalf of Mike and to describe his competent, responsible work performance at the hospital.

Both the supervisor and I believed Mike was innocent. He had money with him that night to pay for the umbrella. If he had intended to steal it, he would hardly have walked through the store with the price tag visibly attached to it.

Moreover, during the past year there was nothing in Mike's behavior to indicate that he would give up all he had going for him—a job, an excellent parole status, a new life—for an umbrella and a possible prison sentence. It just didn't make sense. I remembered how many times I had been in similar situations and wondered, if I had done what Mike had done, would I have been arrested? This case seemed to be an example of discrimination, perhaps even racially motivated.

The trial was to begin at 10:00 in the morning. Mike, his lawyer and an assistant, Mike's wife, his sister, his work supervisor, and I were all present. The prosecution was supposed to have one witness to substantiate the charge against Mike. By 11:55 the jury had been sworn in for duty, but the prosecution's witness was not in the courtroom. Everyone was dismissed for lunch. At 1:30 the trial resumed. The prosecutor requested a recess. His witness had finally arrived and the two of them left the court room. During the recess, the prosecutor asked Mike's lawyer to confer with him, after which the lawyer spoke privately to Mike. Mike returned to the courtroom grinning from ear to ear. He leaned over and whispered, "The witness can't remember anything that happened."

The trial was over and the threat it posed to this innocent man was lifted. But I could not help wondering, was there not a presumption that Mike was guilty because of a past conviction in his life? What would have happened if Mike had not had a supportive group of people available to speak and act on his behalf that day? How strong could this one person have been against the power of prosecution?

POWER IN A RELATIONAL VIEW

Mike Long's story is a story of power. Power is inherent in the dynamics and experience of life. As used here, power is of two kinds. One is linear. Linear power is one-directional. It seeks to achieve its predetermined goal by subordinating and using others to that end. Linear power exploits weaknesses and inequalities and sets up conditions where there are winners and losers.

The other kind of power is relational. Relational power is reciprocal. It seeks to integrate and coordinate others in a process out of which desirable goals emerge. Relational power prizes differences and sets up conditions where everyone feels like a winner.

Most of the events in a person's life are clusterings of many forces and factors. Life moves along as these complex events flow in and out of each other. The values one lives by (e.g., freedom, goodness, peace, beauty, justice, truth) are more or less adequately expressed and experienced in the events which constitute one's life and world. Life is thus characterized by an open relationality among the many events which make up one's life. When this process is occurring well, it generates a kind of relational power or ability to keep relating in an ever more expansive and inclusive manner.

As described in the narrative, Mike Long was beginning to assemble his life experience in a valuable, relational way: he had a job where he was advancing professionally; he was developing social skills with his peer workers; he was enriching his married life. Mike was feeling good about his life and his ability (power) to keep expanding its scope.

But this process can be disrupted, even halted altogether. When this happens, it often feels like an external force breaking in from outside the usual flow of events which make up one's life experience. Such external events generate a kind of power too. By contrast with the relational power mentioned above, this is a linear power, a force which threatens to take over the direction of one's life and dictate its experience. Such an event occurred in Mike Long's life.

He did what many other persons have done; he stepped outside the store to show his wife the umbrella he intended to buy. In so doing, he also stepped outside the boundary lines others had established. Almost out of nowhere a security guard appeared and a whole different type of power intersected Mike's life movement.

This external event was itself a cluster of many forces, just as most events in our lives are. This cluster of forces exerted a type of linear power. First of all, there was the power of the store's security system. Undoubtedly, the officer in question was doing what he was supposed to do—watch for theft. The way he carried out his duty, however, reflected the exercise of linear power, especially with the quick arrest, handcuffing, and transport to jail. The officer could have simply asked Mike, for example, why he had left the store with the umbrella, or at least given him a chance to discuss the situation. That would have been more relational. Instead, this one person and this one event generated a kind of power which took control of Mike's life.

A second source of linear power in this story was the court system by which bail was set, hearing and trial dates determined, and the process for adjudication (lawyers and jury) prearranged. Mike had no say or influence in all of this. The judicial system was injected into his life and he had to adjust. In a more relational approach, the incident need not have gone to the court system at all.

A third source of linear power was Mike's past criminal record, accompanied by a whole social attitude toward ex-offenders. A past crime is often taken as justification for assuming present (repeated) crimes. Rather than this event being seen on its own terms (the relational way), it was subsumed under the power of a particular past which was always liable to reassert itself.

Finally, there may have been a fourth source of linear power—racism. If Mike had not been black, the security officer may have treated him differently, given him the benefit of the doubt, merely asked for an explanation rather than arresting and handcuffing him.

While other aspects of linear power in this case could be cited, these are sufficient to indicate that such an external event is not simply an isolated or trivial fact. It is a powerful source of many forces which threaten the current flow of one's relational life. Linear power must always be dealt with.

In a relational view, the ideal is to absorb the force of linear power into one's own set of relationships so as to maintain control of one's life and reduce the threat of outside forces. When this is possible, which is not always the case, it requires time and effort and the exercise of a greater relational power.

That is what Mike had to do. His arrest threatened to rearrange the pattern of his relationships. If he was to absorb it into his own chosen pattern, he was going to have to gather his own relational power.

This process began when his family posted bail. In doing so, they reasserted the power of his familial relationship. Then Mike enlisted the support of his employer and of me as the LEEO director. By our very presence in the courtroom, we professionals testified to Mike's wider relational life and the value it represented. We were, of course, a source of personal support and encouragement to Mike but more than that we brought *his* larger world into the courtroom. Thus situated, we helped Mike absorb the linear power of his arrest and the other forces contained in that event.

The hope is that when linear power meets relational power, the former is swallowed up in the larger, deeper, richer experience of relationships. In this case, that hope was realized almost visibly when the witness withdrew and the prosecution's other reinforcements vanished as well.

But what if Mike had not had his family, his employer, and the rest of us with him? What if he had tried to compete on a linear basis with his accusers? No doubt, their linear power would have won. But if that had happened, neither Mike nor society would have benefited because the possibilities for each to establish expanding relationships would have been canceled. What would have canceled them was a power that in one sense was protecting public interest (security and court systems) but in another sense was perpetuating public prejudices (stereotypes about criminals and racism).

The lesson which emerges from this story is that liberation is an exercise of power. The most liberating power that can be exercised is relational. When external events intervene and threaten to close off relational possibilities and control a person's life development from the outside (instead of control remaining inside, with the person), then a greater response of relational power is necessary.

Even when this is done successfully, it is successful only for that particular event. Each new moment brings its own opportunities and its own threats. Mike absorbed the linear power in this case, but he will have to keep strengthening his own relational power in order to keep liberating himself, his family, his society.

POWER IN A CHRISTIAN VIEW

Mike Long's story reenacts the experience of power in a Christian view of life. The confrontation of powers frames the story of human salvation, and God is right in the middle of it. At first glance, many biblical stories seem to depict God using linear power. This impression is especially given in stories where God is described as punishing people (e.g., in the story of the flood at the time of Noah, Gen. 7–10; the plagues in Egypt at the time of Moses, Exod. 7–12; the exile of Israel at the time of the Assyrians and Babylonians as well as the persecution of the Jews by the Romans, books of the Maccabees).

But a closer reading of those stories shows that God's exercise of power, however graphically and dramatically it is portrayed, is for the purpose of the covenant (Gen. 9, 15; Exod. 19; Jer. 7; 2 Sam. 7). And the covenant is the supremely relational experience in the Jewish and Christian religious tradition. Through the covenant, God establishes an inseparable bond with human beings, beginning with the Jewish people but expanding through time to include all people.

The covenant is not a linear agreement. Its initiative comes from God but its fulfillment only comes as human persons choose to enter and maintain the covenantal relationship which God offers. And human persons are often reluctant, resistant, defiant about entering this relationship. Because of human, linear power exerted against God, God's response may initially appear, or be described, as linear in kind. But it is not.

It is a manifestation of God's relational power which is real power, not passivity, and is commensurate with the opposing linear power which it seeks to absorb and transform. Now, Christians believe that God's way of relating to human persons is most fully revealed in Jesus. As the gospel versions of his life are presented, they are full of power confrontations. Some of these are described in the familiar, conventional style of the Jewish Scriptures as confrontations with unknown evil forces, like the expulsion of demons from a man in Gerasa (Mark 5:1-20) or with clearly known opposition, like the money changers and traders in the temple area (John 2:13-17).

But like the God whom he called Father, Jesus exercised his power for the fulfillment of the covenant, or as he preferred to describe it, for the coming of the reign of God. Either expression made clear that relationship with God was the all-important aim. Everything else had to be related to that. But maintaining such a priority and relationship was not easy, was not automatic, and was not accomplished once and for all.

In fact, Jesus struggled to maintain his relational power right up to the end of his life. In the stylized debate with Pilate which is recorded in John's gospel (John 18:28–19:16), Jesus kept trying to open Pilate to the possibility of a different experience. Pilate seemed intrigued by the discussion about kingship (John 18:33-37) but cut off the dialogue when Jesus introduced the question of truth (John 18:38).

Pilate made some attempts to satisfy the accusers of Jesus by having him scourged, but this didn't work. He was matching linear power with linear power and he was losing (there are always winners and losers with linear power). When he resumed his discussion with Jesus, Jesus wouldn't enter in. Frustrated, Pilate resorted to a linear approach. "Do you not know that I have the power to release you and the power to crucify you?"

Jesus responded relationally. "You would have no power over me whatever unless it were given you from above." He put power back into its proper relationship, an ability given by God to create relationships that are life-giving. Those who use this ability for another purpose—to control, to dominate, to interfere—are the ones who are really in trouble. "That is why he who handed me over to you is guilty of the greater sin" (John 19:11).

John's gospel observes that "after this, Pilate was eager to release him." He was almost led into a relational experience, but in the end the influence of linear power was too great. "Pilate handed Jesus over to be crucified."

Jesus' crucifixion seemed to say that linear power had triumphed over the relational possibilities Jesus represented. But in a Christian view just the opposite is the case. Belief in Jesus' resurrection (an explicitly Christian interpretation) or an acknowledgment of the new, life-giving energy his death stimulated (a broadly Christian-humanist interpretation) assert that linear power did not triumph in that instance. Nor will it ever triumph if it is confronted by a relational power adequate to the challenge. Jews in history and Jesus in his life have shown their relational power adequate to the challenge. So did Mike Long. And so must everyone who tries to liberate power for the sake of life.

Liberating Self-Perception

THE STORY

RENEE LEWIS WAS TRYING. She had been admitted into the LEEO program on June 20, 1978. Renee was twenty-one years old and a high school graduate. She was on one-year probation, having been convicted of mail fraud.

When Renee arrived at the LEEO office for her first appointment, she brought her ten-month-old child, Frederick, with her. During the initial screening session, it was obvious that she would require a great deal of support. As with most of the women who have been through the court and prison systems, her sense of self-worth and self-confidence had been significantly damaged.

She had experienced shame in adjusting to family and friends following her conviction. She alone was responsible to care for Frederick because she had no financial assistance or caring support from Frederick's father.

In contacting prospective employers on behalf of Renee, the LEEO staff had attempted to identify a job that would be within a small working environment. This would reduce possible stress and limit the number of interactions with co-workers. The owner of an exclusive dress shop in the Georgetown area of Washington, D.C., expressed a willingness to hire Renee. He was unconcerned that she had a criminal conviction and felt that an initial interview was unnecessary. He wanted her to begin immediately and he agreed to train her in the sale of dresses. His requirements were that she be pleasant to customers and agreeable in following directions.

Renee had been prepared for her first day of work and expressed excitement and hope in the prospect of having found her long-awaited job. She arrived promptly for work, but within the hour the employer was on the phone with me, angrily shouting, "Why did you ever send someone so stupid to me?"

I asked to speak to Renee. Renee came to the phone obviously upset and crying. She explained that she had tried to do exactly as the employer had asked, but she apparently was not the type of person he was looking for. She was advised to return to the LEEO office to talk further about the incident. When the employer picked up the phone again, he said, "I don't think she could even fill a bag with french fries at a McDonald's restaurant."

Before coming to the LEEO program, Renee had completed a training program in sales work and bookkeeping procedures. She had had prior work experience at a large department store, the General Services Administration, and had served as a staff member for a youth services program. Yet, she simply didn't believe she could make it, and she didn't. The impression formed by the employer was not the result of Renee's professional incompetence; it was rather the result of her lack of self-confidence and assertiveness. She was trapped by her own poor self-perception and couldn't liberate herself from it.

SELF-PERCEPTION IN A RELATIONAL VIEW

The story of Renee is the story of self-perception. Each person has a self-image which is developed largely through a series of interactions between the individual and other persons. In addition, a person's self-image is drawn from and projected onto a larger perception of what people in general are supposed to be like. So, there is a constant flow of experience shaping the actual process of a person's self-perception.

The heart of this process is a uniquely internal activity by which each person takes in a selection of the many experiences swirling about in the environment and combines these experiences with other elements like values, ideals, goals, hopes, etc. Thus, a person's self-image emerges out of the uniquely personal interplay between the stubborn, hard facts of reality and the fluid, novel possibilities of thought.

There is no automatic, predetermined outcome in this process. Each person is self-creating. What ordinarily happens, however, is that the hard facts of reality have a more powerful influence on a person's self-perception than do the imaginative possibilities of creative reflection. Human persons are primarily feeling beings and the strongest, most influential feelings come from what has already, actually entered one's experience rather than from what could potentially enter one's experience.

This is especially true when the immediate social environment in which a person develops does not generate many possibilities or encouragement for new experience. In that case the cycle of repetition is much harder to change and the possibilities for a different sort of experience are severely reduced. Even then, change can occur but it requires extraordinary imagination and self-assertion to become anything different from what a person is conditioned to be because of the way one's social environment is structured. This is the basis for the self-fulfilling prophecy that mocks any attempt to act on new possibilities and become a new type of person.

When a social environment exerts this kind of controlling influence, it harms not only the individuals within it but the creative advance of societal life itself. For life aims at maximizing possibilities for new experience. These possibilities arise from an imaginative rethinking and reenacting of what has already happened. But if the imaginative, the novel, the possible dimension of life itself is cut off or so reduced by the social environment that its influence is negligible, then life as a whole suffers—as do the individuals who constitute it.

In the preceding story, Renee was caught in such a limiting social environment. Her self-image and the possibilities for its creative development were drastically restricted by the actual experience which not only defined her past but threatened to dictate her future. In three ways especially her social environment controlled her self-image.

First was the discrepancy in the way society perceives female ex-offenders in contrast to male ex-offenders. Women are not supposed to commit crime, whereas if men commit crime, it is understandable, even acceptable in an ironic sense. Most of the male ex-offenders who came through the LEEO program were significantly influenced as children by male role models in their homes and neighborhoods. Usually, their fathers, older brothers, or other blood relatives had been incarcerated. The same factors which led to antisocial and criminal behavior in their relatives continued to influence them: substandard living conditions, inadequate and inferior education, lack of job opportunities with upward mobility. Given these conditions, the perpetuation of crime among males was predictable and therefore neither surprising nor especially demeaning when it occurred.

Not so with the women who came through the LEEO program. Although they grew up in the same social environment as men, they were not supposed to be influenced by it to the point of engaging in antisocial or criminal behavior. And most of the time, they really didn't. Their offenses were acting as an accomplice (e.g., being in the car) with a male who actually committed the crime; writing bad checks (which they may have been told were good or which they were set up to write); making a drug drop or picking up a payment (sometimes without knowing what was really going on).

The social environment expected women to be supportive of their men but not to get caught, and certainly not to get convicted. If they did go to prison, they not only faced the prison sentence but they awaited an equally painful experience of shame, guilt, and sometimes rejection by their families upon release.

The second way Renee's social environment controlled her self-image was in regard to her child. Children are considered the responsibility of women, not of men. If the man is incarcerated, the woman assumes the responsibility of providing for the children as well as raising them. But if the woman is incarcerated, the reverse is not usually the case. At least among LEEO participants, the children would often be spread among various family members.

Sometimes, while in prison, the women did not even know who had their children, much less how they were doing. In addition to the personal anxiety this created, it also meant that it would be that much more difficult for the women after they were released from prison to relate to their children. Their readjustment from the cell to society was compounded by the way the children would often blame their mothers for having left them or for causing them any pain while they were incarcerated.

As if this weren't enough, while a female ex-offender would be seeking a job (or even after she found employment), she faced the added burden of providing day care for her children and having to respond to emergencies, illness, etc. By fulfilling her responsibilities as a mother, she could jeopardize her possibilities as an employee. Male ex-offenders in the LEEO program rarely had this double dilemma to contend with.

The third way Renee's social environment controlled her self-image was in the impact of incarceration and the expectations of the female ex-offender after release from prison. The female ex-offenders in the LEEO program experienced incarceration to be extremely dehumanizing. They seemed to internalize the feelings of worthlessness and dependency which the prison system tended to engender. Once released, they were expected not to talk about the experience and not to seek help in dealing with it but to pick up and get on with life.

As a result, women like Renee need a great deal of support, reinforcement, encouragement, and affirmation. They have many suppressed feelings and adopt a passive, restrained demeanor that can be interpreted as indifference or incompetence. This clearly is not helpful in seeking and retaining employment and it caught up with Renee.

Whatever prompted the owner of the dress shop to react as he did, the effect was to crush the attempts which Renee had been making with LEEO's help to construct a new self-image for herself. The employer's curt, offensive dismissal of her opened the door through which all the previous social conditioning came rushing in. The hopeful prospects which were being gently assembled were no match for the impact of society's perception of Renee. The rejection, humiliation, and failure which gripped her after that incident became a self-fulfilling prophecy instead of a self-creating possibility.

The lesson which emerges from this story is that liberation includes self-perception. The focus is on each individual, but the individual shapes a self-image largely out of the reality of the environment in which he or she lives. The social environment can be a powerful (linear) force which induces individuals to conform to its dominant influence. This can restrict freedom and creativity on the part of the individual. When this happens, a greater concentration of effort is needed to support and facilitate individuals to become their most creative selves.

This effort in turn helps liberate society, because the large social environment is the accumulation of all the experiences which the individuals feed into it. The freer and more creative those individual experiences are, the freer and more creative will the social environment become. And when that happens, life itself is enhanced.

SELF-PERCEPTION IN A CHRISTIAN VIEW

The story of Renee reenacts a basic motif in the Christian view of life. Those who are called to play a special role in the scheme of salvation (and who fulfill their own potential in the process) usually do so against the backdrop of powerful counterforces in their social environment. But God is not controlled by social expectations and does not necessarily abide by them. This pattern is found in the sources of both Jewish and Christian tradition, and it has special poignancy in the case of women.

Despite the dominant, patriarchal character of society in biblical times (and the dominant, patriarchal caste to the telling of biblical stories), God consistently challenges people to change (convert) their self-perception and see themselves as God sees them. This occurs especially in the story of women like Hagar, the maidservant who gave birth to

Ishmael (Gen. 16:1-16), Pharaoh's daughter who saved Moses (Exod. 2:1-10), Deborah who was a judge in Israel and whose canticle is one of the earliest and best examples of Hebrew poetry (Judges 4–5). Entire books are written about Ruth, a non-Jew whose fidelity to her mother-in-law was a model for Jewish virtue; Judith, whose trust in God saved her people; Esther, whose story explains the origin and meaning of the Jewish feast of Purim.

This pattern continues into the Christian story. Mary, the mother of Jesus, maintains her self-perception as disclosed to her by God's messenger against the judgment of others (Matt. 1:18-25; Luke 1:26-38). The penitent woman insists on honoring Jesus at a Pharisee's house even though she was generally considered to be a sinner (Luke 7:36-50). Mary, the sister of Martha, breaks custom and converses with Jesus rather than do the expected, household chores, for which she is praised as having chosen "the better portion" (Luke 10:38-42). And, of course, the first witnesses to Jesus' resurrection are the women who alone remained faithful to him in his death and whose testimony would carry no legal weight in public (Matt. 28:1-7; Mark 16:1-8; Luke 24:1-12; John 20:1-18).

Perhaps the clearest, certainly the most detailed, example of Jesus' offering a new self-perception to a woman occurs in John 4:4-42. While passing through a Samaritan town, Jesus paused for a rest. He was waiting for his disciples to return with some food when a Samaritan woman came by the well to draw water. Jesus began to speak with her, which conflicted with two customs: Jews didn't speak to Samaritans and men did not ordinarily address women in public.

The conversation which ensued is clearly an editorialized teaching which covers the basic sacramental positions of the early Christians regarding baptism (John 4:7-15), the true spirit of worship (4:19-24), and eucharist (4:31-38). But this incident also reflects others in which Jesus saw in people what they could be and not simply what the social environment determined them to be. Jesus was not oblivious to social perceptions but he was not controlled by them either. At the end of his encounter with the Samaritan woman, she had become his messenger, bringing to her townsfolk (many of whom no doubt ostracized her for her five marriages) the message, "Come and see someone who has told me everything I ever did. Could this not be the Messiah?" (4:29). Indeed, John's gospel notes, "Many Samaritans from that town believed in him on the strength of the woman's word of testimony" (4:39).

In this instance as in so many others Jesus liberated people by reaching deep into the inner life of each person and challenging them to claim the freest, most creative, and truest image of themselves. When they did so, they began to experience themselves and to interact in their environment in new ways. And that process began to liberate their society as well.

It does not always work this way, of course. It didn't work completely in the case of Renee. But success ratios are not the motive for living in either a relational or a Christian view of life. Rather, the motivation is to liberate one another, to help others see and enact their best self-image. When that happens, not only the individual but society itself is liberated one more time.

CHAPTER FOUR

Liberating Systems

THE STORY

ROBERT JAMES WAS GIVEN A CHANCE. On August 12, 1982, he was admitted into the LEEO program. While still incarcerated at the Lorton, Virginia, Reformatory, Robert was permitted to attend the LEEO job readiness sessions twice a week. He would be eligible for parole if he could find suitable employment. Once employed, he could be released from prison.

On September 23, 1982, Robert was hired as a full-time maintenance worker with a starting salary of $5.50 an hour. The firm which hired Robert had a maintenance contract to provide janitorial services within government buildings. The firm had worked cooperatively with LEEO before and had hired a number of job-ready ex-felons. Moreover, it evidenced a high level of responsibility in placing these persons in government work sites. Careful supervision of these individuals was conducted by LEEO staff members in cooperation with the employee's work supervisor.

There was only one problem. A government regulation required a review of all government buildings by the Office of Federal Protective Service Management. Even though persons employed through LEEO had been carefully screened prior to job placement and were under close supervision while working, they were not exempt from an investigation by the Federal Protective Agency.

On several occasions when this type of investigation was made, it had led to the job termination of LEEO employees, some of whom had been employed from six to twelve months. In every instance the termination was the result of past convictions in the employee's history—a fact well known to the firm which hired them. LEEO had tried to overrule these decisions to terminate its participants. Letters of support from the individuals' employers, letters from the LEEO board chairman and program director, as well as hundreds of phone calls on behalf of the persons being terminated usually had no effect. There was no current criminal behavior by the employee to warrant this termination from employment. In one instance, the employer remarked, "I hate to lose this employee. He's the best worker I have ever had."

On March 17, 1983, Robert was informed of his job termination. The letter, forwarded to his employer, stated, "We have been advised by the Office of Federal Protective Service Management that your below named employee is unsuitable for work under your cleaning contract. . . . You must immediately exclude the employee from any work in such areas."

The afternoon he received this news, Robert visited the LEEO office. He manifested a high level of frustration and depression at having been fired from his job. Everyone was concerned for him. The next day LEEO received a phone call from a staff person at the halfway house where Robert resided.

Robert had been found dead that morning. He had died from a self-administered overdose of drugs. There was no question that Robert had taken his life in response to the news of his firing. Having lived for what he wanted to be in the present, he had died for what he had done in the past.

The LEEO staff was stunned and angry. They felt they had to take some action to prevent this type of tragedy from happening again. But help was needed. I contacted Mr. Chris Gordon, a newsreporter for a local TV station, who was familiar with LEEO. On March 24 he aired Robert's story. In addition, we contacted Mr. William Raspberry of the *Washington Post*. He had previously written two editorials on LEEO and now on March 28 he wrote another editorial describing Robert's job termination and subsequent death.

The media were effective. Representatives from both the General Services Administration and the Office of Federal Protective Service Management were willing to schedule meetings to discuss the serious consequences of Robert's job termination and possible solutions to the problem. The problem was rooted in the existing policy and efforts to change it seemed futile. However, after persistent meetings, an appointment was scheduled with the Commissioner for Public Buildings Service and his staff.

It was anticipated that this would be "just another meeting" in which concern would be the token and rhetoric would be the outcome. Such was not the case. It was apparent from the outset of the meeting that the commissioner intended to introduce an alternative for the

LEEO program to the current government policy. He was clearly impressed with the quality of services being offered to both the LEEO employee and employer. At his recommendation, the following letter was issued for public dissemination:

> This is to inform you that the Public Buildings Service has established a pilot program for ex-offenders who are certified by the LEEO Program as eligible for employment by our custodial and service contractors. Special procedures have been set up for these applicants. As the primary industry in Washington, D.C., the Federal Government represents a major mechanism for ex-offenders who are screened and ready to reenter the labor force. We are encouraged by the excellent record which LEEO has established in this area and are looking forward to the successful implementation of this pilot program.

While Robert's death had been a tragedy, it had not been in vain. It resulted in a change in government policy and a curbing of the power of discrimination.

SYSTEMS IN A RELATIONAL VIEW

This story centers on Robert's life and death, but his story cannot be told without including the stories of many other persons (his employer, the LEEO supervisors, media personnel, representatives of government agencies) and many systems which structured his life (the corrections system, the cleaning firm he worked for, government, LEEO, public news media). As already noted, every person's life is constituted by the confluence of many events. The ideal is to direct the process of one's own life as fully and as freely as possible. This means that each person selects from all the influences impinging on a given occasion those which would constitute the fullest possible experience of being alive. This selection process is an exercise of freedom and self-determination. In the present story, Robert seemed to be taking control of his own life process in a more satisfying way than he had previously.

While in prison, he was able (and willing) to begin job readiness training at LEEO. Then he had to go on interviews for an actual job. Finally, when he was hired, he had to perform well on the work site. At each step, Robert had to choose what he would do and who he would become. He had to choose from a number of other possibilities (becoming dependent, returning to crime, taking a less demanding job) in order to shape his life the way he did.

Out of these multiple possibilities and decisions the general character or form of one's life emerges. Usually some factor dominates and tends to organize everything else systematically in relation to itself. For example, at one point Robert's life was dominated by the fact of crime he had committed. That put the stamp on his life as a whole. Then, after he was released from prison and began working, employment became the dominant character of his life. Some experiences were related to it (like self-esteem, productivity, good peer relationships, a measure of independence) while other experiences were excluded from it (like self-pity, idleness, manipulative relationships, dependency). And many more potential experiences could be envisioned which gave purpose and appeal to Robert's future.

The segment of Robert's story which was told above is only part of his total life experience. But that segment, like every other, has its dominant character which systematizes the events which defined his life at that time. The dominant character in this instance is his death. Not just death in general, as a fact of human experience, but Robert's death. That means, it is the death which characterizes his experience, which assembles the many other events in his life in the unique way that determines who he had become.

This unique, personal quality is found in every event which constitutes a person's life. It is the distinctive, inexplicable, novel aspect of every experience. Human persons are able to speak in generalities, using abstract terms (like *crime, employment, death*) or collective references (like *criminals, government, representatives, media, staff*), but life is not lived that way. Life is made up of specific events, particular episodes which are always one of a kind, even if they are similar to other events or are repeated in one's own life experience.

This quality of uniqueness is often found in the contrasting features of each event. Contrasts are the people, the feelings, the values, the experiences which are related to the dominant character of an event and give it its own particular intensity or novelty or meaning. In Robert's case there were several contrasts which entered into the event of his death and gave it its peculiar character.

There was, first of all, the shocking news that he was to be "immediately excluded" from his job. This word stood in stark contrast to his previous inclusion in the work force, where he had performed very well. In addition, the decision came from a system, from a routine check of records, and was conveyed in a matter-of-fact, bureaucratic manner. This also stood in contrast to the personal, caring way Robert had been treated by the LEEO staff and by his employer. Robert undoubtedly felt these events more as contradictions to or reversals of his current experience than as contrasts. In any event, they contributed directly to his death.

At the same time, the system of the Federal Protective Service Management was doing its job. There is a public trust to be protected and security to be supervised. The employees of the Federal Protective Agency were not acting illegally or unethically. Nonetheless, their action represented a stark contrast to the reality of Robert's situation. He had become a trusted, dependable worker. If the security system had checked the employer, not just the record, it may have decided differently. But that was not the procedure. As a result, an external, contrasting factor entered Robert's experience which he chose to relate to by taking his own life.

The strongest contrast of all surely occurred within Robert himself. He was overcoming his past mistakes, beginning to orient himself and use the resources in his environment more productively, trying to create a new image and feeling about himself. In contrast to this emerging, positive identity, Robert's depression the day he received his termination notice was overpowering. It was as if he were being torn in two directions at once, and he chose to follow neither path.

None of these contrasts necessitated Robert's death. He chose to act as he did in relation to all that was happening. But at the same time, there was a system of factors that seemed out of his control, and they were dominating him at that moment and threatening to dictate his future as well. Taking these factors into account, one could say that Robert did not simply die; he was victimized.

And yet, no one in particular was clearly the victimizer. If Robert's whole life were laid out, one could point to certain events, conditions, influences, people, decisions that shaped Robert's experience. One could spell out more accurately where the dominant character of his life and death came from. But such analysis would not change the actual life and death experience which was Robert's.

However, it could have influence in another way. No one is in complete control of the factors which impact one's life, but this does not mean persons are merely receptive or passive. What they do with the influences they receive from the world around them also has an impact on that same world. A person's decisions, experiences, life process both draws from and returns to the larger system of events which make up the world as a whole. No one can completely control this phase of one's life either. In fact, the greatest impact of one's life (apart from one's own interior experience) is sometimes what others do with the events and experience one generates.

This was certainly true in Robert's case. His death had a very dramatic and powerful impact on others, especially the LEEO staff. It was not acceptable to them that he was victimized; something had to be done about it. As they felt his death experience, with all of its contrasts and forces, they were stimulated to give it a new meaning, to put Robert's death in relation to other experiences and events and people and thus to redefine his death and give it a new role in the system of shaping life in the environment where he and they existed.

There were many ways in which this could be attempted. But LEEO went to its own dominant character—liberation. The question posed by Robert's death was: What does liberation mean now, in these circumstances? In view of Robert's death how can LEEO become what it should be, a liberative agent for ex-offenders in society? The specific steps which were taken are described in the story itself. In each instance the impact of Robert's death was being extended because that experience had become part of someone else's experience. And the bonding of these experiences was empowering and influential. The result of this particular process can be seen in three ways.

First of all, Robert's memory was liberated. He was not just a victim, a person who couldn't take adversity and who chose an easy way out. He became an impetus and a means for liberation. Because of him, changes occurred, which opened up new and more promising possibilities for others.

Second, public policy was liberated. The automatic exclusion of particular ex-felons was rescinded, at least for those who were in the LEEO program. It remains a bit of a mystery why the commissioner for Public Buildings Service ruled as he did. But it is clear that if LEEO had not determined to act on Robert's death, no change in the system would have taken place.

Third, future workers were liberated. As a result of the policy change, LEEO participants who might work in government buildings in the future would not be fired because they are ex-felons. They need not know why they have this security. In fact, when one LEEO participant, who now works in a government building, was asked if he had ever heard of Robert, he said no. He didn't have to. His own freedom had been freely assured. Robert was part of this man's current experience whether he knew it or not.

This is the relational view of life that has guided LEEO's liberative efforts. Everyone is engaged in an open process of becoming, individually and collectively. Every event has its own particular character and contributes to the overall character and structure of life together. As people feel each other's experience, they receive it and give back to the whole their own unique construction of that experience. This is a creative and dynamic process. It can be liberating as well, not just for individuals but for the systems of society.

SYSTEMS IN A CHRISTIAN VIEW

Robert's story reenacts the central event in a Christian view of life. Death need not be the mere termination of life. It can, in fact, generate new life which liberates both individuals and the social systems in which they live. The difference between a terminal death and a liberative death is expressed in the difference between the terms *victim* and *sacrifice*. Both are prominent in the Jewish and Christian tradition.

A victim is helpless, completely under the (linear) power of others, with no identity (self-perception) or value except in the role assigned by those who dominate. For a human being to be a victim is a tragedy and to be a "victim of circumstances" of nameless, impersonal, systemic forces is an ultimate tragedy.

A sacrifice, on the other hand, is deliberate, for the sake of (in relation to) others, with a value derived from the effects of the sacrifice which are not clearly perceived but are consciously hoped for. A sacrifice links people with one another and with a superior force, thus strengthening the system of togetherness which characterizes life. A sacrifice is honorable, and to be a sacrifice for the world is salvific.

Sacrifice played an important role in Jewish experience. Before an impending crisis or after a turning point in the history of salvation, sacrifice was offered. There were many kinds of sacrificial "victims" (animals, grain, fruits) and many forms of sacrifice (burnt offerings, holocausts) for different purposes (peace, gratitude, atonement), but in every instance sacrifice represented a conscious strengthening of the bonds (systems) which held people's lives together. Moreover, human beings were never included among the sacrificial victims.

This did not mean, however, that human beings could not offer their lives on behalf of others, even to the point of death if need be. The clearest example of such voluntary self-sacrifice is described in Isaiah

42, 49, 50, and 52, where the suffering servant of the Lord is extolled as the Savior of Israel.

This image formed the backdrop for narrating the suffering and death of Jesus, just as the larger tradition of sacrifice formed the backdrop for interpreting the meaning of his death (in the letter to the Hebrews, for example). Jesus' death was the pivotal event in his life. On the surface of it (as already noted in chapter two) his death seemed to be terminal and he appeared to be a victim of a superior linear power. But the Christian view of Jesus' death sees it differently.

Jesus chose to die for the sake of others in order to empower them to face and overcome the forces that threaten them with terminal death. This was not an easy choice for Jesus to make nor did he make it entirely on his own volition. All the gospels make it clear that Jesus acted in response to what he perceived as God's will for him (Jesus' own self-perception despite what his social environment was telling him). This is most graphically conveyed in his agony before being arrested (Matt. 26:36-46; Mark 14:32-42; Luke 22:40-46) and also while he hung on the cross (Matt. 27:45-50; Mark 15:33-36).

However, Jesus remained in control of his death. This is emphatically portrayed in John's gospel (chapters 18–19) where Jesus is really in charge of those who arrest him (18:1-9), guides the inquiry before the high priest (18:19-24), and shapes the trial dialogue with Pilate (18:28–19:16). Even on the cross, he makes provision for his mother (19:26-27), fulfills a prophecy (19:28-30), and only then dies.

The value of his death, like the value of any sacrifice, was not clearly perceived at the time. But as that value became clear, it was narrated in the appearance stories which conclude each of the gospels and in the chronicle of his disciples' mission recorded in the Acts of the Apostles. Over and over again the proclamation is that his death has freed all people. Thus freed, they are able to give themselves to others. A new process is generated whereby persons who enter into his death experience (whether consciously or not) are empowered to enter also his new life and to draw the world they relate to into that same, new life.

When Robert died, he died as a victim. But his death had the potential of becoming sacrificial, of becoming a reenactment of the death-resurrection experience of Jesus. It was not clear from the outset what this might mean practically. But when Robert's death was consciously united with the value of liberation (expressed in the death-resurrection experience of Jesus), a new power was generated. Robert was transformed into more than a victim, and his death into more than a personal tragedy.

To liberate is to change systems which harm people. Death is the ultimate harm which any system can effect. When Robert died as a victim of the system he was in, LEEO had to act. It did so out of its basic relational view of life as well as its explicit Christian convictions. Both sources provided support and guidance for what LEEO did, and both confirmed that even in the experience of death, there is power for change and new life. One must be willing to invest deeply in that experience if the potential for change is to be realized. When LEEO invested itself, a victim became a sacrifice.

CHAPTER FIVE

Liberating Judgment

THE STORY

ROGER BOND WAS READY TO START OVER. He had been convicted of mail fraud and forged securities. After completing his prison sentence at the Federal Prison Camp at Allenwood, Pennsylvania, he was on parole.

Roger was admitted into the LEEO program on November 15, 1983. While in the program, he completed and often exceeded the LEEO job readiness and pre-employment requirements. Roger was an unusual job candidate. Unlike most of the LEEO participants, he had extensive past work experience, an impressive work history, and a college degree. Yet these very qualifications were a handicap when he sought suitable work, because he also had a criminal record. Between December 8, 1983, and January 23, 1984, Roger was interviewed by five prospective employers, including national research institutes, a transit authority, and a large electronics firm. Seeking high-level employment positions in prestigious firms meant that Roger had to pass security clearance and provide the prospective employer with satisfactory character references. His past criminal conviction seriously impaired Roger's efforts to establish his credibility.

By February 3, 1984, Roger and the LEEO staff agreed that it would be best for him to leave the program and obtain a hacker's license (to drive a cab). In this way he would at least have a steady source of income and a flexible work schedule which would enable him to pursue his own job development in the professional fields of his choice. LEEO would continue to offer references on his behalf to any prospective employers he would identify as well as offer advice and direction to Roger in his efforts to develop job leads.

Roger applied for his hacker's license, but on March 8, 1984, he received a letter from the Government of the District of Columbia, Public Vehicles Branch, notifying him that his application for a license to operate a public vehicle had been denied. The reason was that he "was on parole for the crimes of mail fraud and falsely made or forged securities and that because these crimes involved public trust, Mr. Bond is not of good moral character."

The wording expressed a paralyzing judgment: he *was* convicted and therefore *is* not of good moral character. Not only was the statement grammatically incorrect, it was also condemnatory in its assumption. Could a person be convicted, serve the imposed sentence, satisfy parole requirements, and make sincere efforts to become a self-reliant, responsible citizen, but never again be of good moral character? Was it not possible that a person who once had demonstrated behaviors that clearly signified an inappropriate moral character could at a future time demonstrate behaviors that signified a good moral character?

With the help of an attorney, Roger appealed the decision. On April 26, 1984, a meeting was scheduled with the District of Columbia Hacker's License Appeal Board. Present for this meeting were Roger, his attorney, members of the License Appeal Board and a representative from the Public Vehicles Branch.

I was requested to offer testimony on behalf of Mr. Bond. In my testimony I pointed out the discrepancy in the decision to deny Mr. Bond a license. Clearly, the denial was based on past behaviors and not on present achievements. Roger's personal efforts toward rehabilitation were enumerated and spoke for themselves. It became a simple matter of focus. In making a judgment that will affect a person's tomorrows should one dwell on the past or the present? Since his release from prison, Roger had demonstrated responsible decision making within the social community which fit the requirements for the operator of a public vehicle.

The board questioned Roger. Why, if he had a college degree, was he applying for a hacker's license? Roger responded out of his struggle. For many months he had attempted to find a job. Although some of the companies appeared to have no openings at the time of his application, he felt his criminal conviction was most often the key factor in not obtaining employment. In his judgment, having a license would give him the self-confidence of being employed, and this would offset the feelings of discouragement and frustration that come with being unemployed. With a renewed sense of dignity and accomplishment, he could then better pursue his efforts toward gainful employment.

On May 15, 1984, Roger received a letter from the Appeals Board. The board had heard his story, felt his struggle, believed in his vision.

"The Board finds that Mr. Bond's conduct since his release from prison has been satisfactory and that Mr. Bond's efforts in rehabilitating himself have shown that Mr. Bond is of 'good moral character.' Therefore, the Board's decision is to overrule the decision of the Public Vehicles Branch in denying Mr. Bond a license and grant Mr. Bond his appeal."

JUDGMENT IN A RELATIONAL VIEW

Roger Bond's story is a story of judgment. His life, like everyone's, is constituted by the multiple relationships he enters into. These relationships, in turn, consist of numerous, individual events which together make up his life as a whole. These events are not simply experienced; they are also judged.

Judgment implies a ranking or arranging of events, experiences, persons. How a person judges or arranges the experiences in one's life largely determines who that person is and how that person relates. Judgments are very determinative and therefore very important.

But they are also very selective. No one can know an event thoroughly. Even the events which constitute one's most private experience are more than anyone can completely grasp. This is partly because each event is a combination of many elements (as described in chapter two) and partly because there are many events occurring simultaneously in one's life. Both the complexity and the quantity of events necessitate a selective judgment.

Judgment orients people to the world which is happening around them and also to the future which they can create. As such, judgment feeds directly into the construction of the relationships and experiences which constitute the world. There is both a personal-individual and a societal-communal dimension in every judgment. And both of these dimensions occur, not primarily at the level of conscious, rational reflection, but at the level of affective, emotional energy.

If judgment were limited to explicit, rational reflection, its impact would be much more definable and controllable than it is. But judgment is not limited in this way. Judgment accompanies every experience. It pervades the way people feel themselves to be part of the world they inhabit, and it pervades the feelings people have about the events and other people which structure their relationship to that world.

Prior to being a logical analysis of the surrounding reality, judgment is a basic feeling of attraction to or distance from that same reality. This is not to say that careful, reflective judgments are not important, or should not be made. Instead, it is to acknowledge that these rather specialized judgments are embedded in a more fundamental network of judging which is very powerful and which links people more deeply to the world than they may ordinarily acknowledge.

As described above, the story of Roger is really the story of three judgments, all about the same reality, simultaneously present, and mutually influencing the construction of this episode in Roger's life. There is, first of all, Roger's own judgment, as evidenced in his decision to leave the LEEO program and seek a hacker's license. This decision, confirmed by the LEEO staff, was prompted by Roger's experience of being turned down for jobs because of his criminal record. He had work experience and a college degree. But these factors made him overqualified for entry-level positions, while his criminal record made him unqualified for positions which required security clearance.

Roger could have carefully analyzed why he found himself caught between these two closed doors, and he could have accurately determined what his chances would be if he were to continue with the same line of pursuit. But there was a deeper judgment operating in his experience. It was the felt conviction that his best future rested in his autonomy. As he told the Appeal Board, he felt that a hacker's license would give him the self-confidence of being employed on his own, which in turn would strengthen his efforts to seek better employment in the future. If he could function on his own, be responsible for his own hours and performance and income, he would have a better chance to create the future for himself that he wanted.

Driving a taxi offered that possibility. In making this decision, Roger felt the importance of his autonomy and kept looking to his future. His self-judgment was that he had a future and it would best be realized by drawing on his surest strength—himself. His judgment and direction were clear, but he needed confirmation from the Public Vehicles Branch of the city government.

This was the second critical judgment in the story. The Public Vehicles Branch looked at Roger's life, just as he had, but selected a different part of it on which to make their judgment. They focused on his past. What they saw there was factual; he had committed crimes involving public trust. Their judgment went no further and was no more inclusive. They envisioned his future as a continuation, if not repetition, of his past.

In so doing, those who passed judgment inevitably confronted Roger's own judgment about his present autonomy and future possibilities. Their conclusion was that what he had been, he would continue to be. No doubt, their judgment was not a carefully reasoned, logical conclusion based on a thorough study of Roger's whole life. The Public Vehicles Branch received numerous requests for hacker's licenses; they developed a set of criteria for making relatively quick decisions, and they acted accordingly.

On the whole, their judgments probably do serve the public interest rather well and reflect a generally reliable pattern of experience in handling such requests. But that's the problem. General patterns, average cases, ordinary criteria do not take the specific circumstances of each case sufficiently into account. And the specific circumstances are what constitute the actual experience being judged. By acting out of routine familiar feelings, the Public Vehicles Branch made a judgment that not only fastened on the past but foreclosed the future.

Except that a third judgment entered the story. Because of Roger's association with LEEO, I was asked to speak on his behalf at the meeting of the License Appeal Board. LEEO had a judgment to make too. It was based not on the past (as the Public Vehicles Branch's judgment was) nor on the future (as Roger's judgment was) but on the present.

The LEEO staff had observed Roger interacting with other participants, had seen him going on job interviews and coping with frustration, had invited him to contribute his expertise on different aspects of the program, and had supported his decision to try obtaining a hacker's license. Moreover, when he decided to appeal the Public Vehicles Branch ruling, he enlisted the help of an attorney and asked LEEO to give testimony, both actions indicating that Roger was convinced of his own judgment and committed to it.

This record of Roger's present behaviors allowed LEEO to speak to the potential he clearly possessed to act in a responsible and trustworthy manner. There were no assurances of course; there never are with human behavior. But there was a deeply felt conviction, based on current evidence, and that was a judgment worth taking into account.

As the story indicates, Roger won his appeal. All three judgments, constructively brought together, called for a fourth. In view of the whole picture, the Appeal Board agreed that the present outweighed the past. In so judging, they opened up a new future for Roger.

Judgment is a crucial factor in a relational view of life. Most people are very engaged in their own activities and respond to other people and events out of a familiar pattern of previous judgments. Even when persons pause and consciously think through a situation in order to formulate a deliberate judgment, they are constantly influenced by feelings from similar events and judge what is going on around and within them very selectively.

The selection may focus on the past, the present, or the future. The tendency is to impose on the present what is felt from the past. The liberative challenge is to focus on the present, without naively discarding the past. In either instance, the future is at stake. And the future is where the best and most creative experience of life can occur, because the future is free to draw upon the present and the past and go beyond them. But this happens only if people's judgments allow the potential of the present to surface and open up the future. The surest way to prevent this is by resting comfortably on the past and judging events backwards. The surest way to enhance it is to engage in liberative judgment.

Roger's story shows what a difference one's judgment can make, not only for an individual but for society, whose future depends on the innumerable judgments being made in the present.

JUDGMENT IN A CHRISTIAN VIEW

Roger's story reenacts the role of judgment in a Christian view of life. In fact, both the Jewish and the Christian Scriptures are full of stories about judgment. These are usually coupled with punishment or reward. A superficial reading of these stories can give the impression that God is a domineering, often angry parent who takes vengeance on the many who deviate and gives rewards to the few who conform to the strict, divine way of life. A closer look offers two important considerations. One is an appreciation of the times in which the Bible was written and of the way in which it was written. When the Bible was written, the autonomy of each person was not judged to be as high a value, in theory or in practice, as it is today.

Today the supression of individual freedom is considered a violation, even though many countries practice it. The same value judgment did not apply in biblical times. People were generally treated collectively in terms of sanctions, threats, rewards, and other tangible outcomes of group behavior. This observation leads to the second consideration.

The authors of the Bible drew upon their own experience to express religious truths. If the leaders of their communities and nations used threats and punishments and sanctions to carry out their judgments, this same characteristic would easily be transferred to God, the supreme leader. That doesn't mean God actually judges (and punishes) in the manner described; it means that one has to read deeper than the description to hear the religious message.

A deeper reading suggests that God's judgment is always fair and future oriented. It is fair because God first makes clear what is expected. Whether this is spelled out in codes of behavior (as in the books of Deuteronomy and Proverbs), or in the lives and teachings of the prophets, or in the practical guidance of Wisdom, Sirach, or in the stories of the righteous and the wicked (e.g., in the books of Samuel, Ezra, Nehemiah, Tobit, etc.), the basis on which God judges is no secret.

What is surprising, however, is that God is not an absolutely impartial judge, applying norms with exact neutrality. God is a merciful judge, prone to be patient, lenient, and oriented toward the future. God's judgment in the present is for the sake of the future. If persons indicate in the present their readiness to live better in the future, God judges (and acts) so as to enhance that possibility. But if persons indicate in the present their refusal to live better in the future, God judges (and acts) so as to change their thinking—sometimes in rather dramatic and harsh ways. But always God's judgment leans toward the future, luring people into a better, more creative, freeing life.

Jesus manifests this same type of judgment. He sometimes invokes the threatening image of divine judgment when confronted with the refusal of people to open themselves to the future he promises. No group caught this judgment more often than the Pharisees (e.g., Mark 7:1-16), presumably because they clung so tightly to their past that they closed off their future.

Most of the time, however, Jesus' judgment is forgiving (though not forgetful) of the past and encouraging for the future. The clearest examples of this are the woman caught in adultery (John 8:1-11), the paralytic (Luke 5:17-26), and the woman who anointed him at Bethany (Mark 14:3-9).

These same themes appear in his parables, like the prodigal son (Luke 15:11-32) and the wicked official who would not forgive as he was forgiven (Matt. 18:21-35). And one of Jesus' last acts was to forgive those who crucified him and to open up a new future to one of the criminals who was executed with him. "I assure you: this day you will be with me in paradise" (Luke 23:43).

The cumulative testimony of Scripture is that God's judgment focuses on the present for the sake of the future. This is the way of liberation; it is God's way.

PART THREE

Caring for Society

THE STORY OF LEEO is more than the story of an idea being put into practice. It is more than the story of an ex-offender job placement program. It is more than the story of a success against discouraging obstacles. It is the story of a social ministry.

As defined in the LEEO experience, social ministry is the attempt to care for society. Caring for society means caring for the people who cannot provide for themselves or who are systematically prevented from taking care of themselves because of the way society is structured. To care for society is to respond to these people by using all the resources available, beginning with the inner resources of those being cared for as well as the resources of society at large. As a result, social ministry cares for individual persons and social systems simultaneously.

Although LEEO's caring for society was inspired and guided by the principles of Christian service, an acceptance of Christianity was not necessary for any individual to share in LEEO's work—nor is acceptance of Christianity necessary to care for society. To care is to invest oneself in another or in society at large because both the individual and society as a whole are worth the investment. And they are worth the investment because everyone is connected to everyone else in a complex set of relationships which ultimately means that the welfare of each is bound up with the welfare of all.

To care is also to know how individuals and systems function. It requires the ability to perceive accurately, analyze thoroughly, and plan realistically. This implies that certain skills must be acquired and developed in order to care for others effectively.

To care is to know one's limits. It is to measure the scope of what one can do and the resources available for doing it. It is to set attainable goals while knowing that the total needs of every person and society go beyond what one can do.

LEEO is an example of caring for society. The question which guides the next two chapters is, what can be learned from LEEO's experience about caring for society? The answer to this question appears in two parts, corresponding to the two parts which define any social ministry. These are the societal environment and the caring persons.

All care takes place in an environment. The environment is not accidental or merely external to the interaction which occurs between persons. Rather the environment enters into the occasion and partially defines what it is going to be. The environment is often overlooked as a factor which shapes the experience of human interaction. This is mainly due to the fact that the interaction between persons is more immediate, more striking, and more central than the environment which serves as background or context.

Clearly a balance between environment and persons is desired. The phrase, *caring for society,* tries to strike that balance. *Caring* is a person-oriented, feeling word while *society* as the object of caring suggests both the persons cared for and also the societal environment in which they live.

In the two chapters which follow, ten general characteristics are listed. These characteristics reflect LEEO's experience of caring for society and are considered transferable to any other example of caring for society. Each characteristic is stated in general terms, illustrated with examples from LEEO's story, and then related to New Testament references. The combination of characteristics from the societal environment and from the caring persons allows the full meaning of LEEO's experience to appear more sharply and faithfully as a caring for society.

CHAPTER SIX

The Societal Environment

1. PLURALISM

IT IS ALMOST A TRUISM to say that we live in a pluralistic society, especially in the United States. It may be debated what this ultimately means and to what degree it is actually true, but pluralism is certainly one of the environmental factors that shapes any activity which seeks to care for society. At the heart of the fact of pluralism is the challenge to affirm and claim one's identity while working with others who have a different identity.

The crucial value here is integrity; the challenge is to forge productive linkages which do not compromise or substitute for one's identity. This is an inevitable task because one cannot care for society adequately without the collaboration of others. In the case of LEEO, many of those "others" did not share a Christian motivation, were not guided explicitly by Christian principles, and did not interpret the outcome of their work as furthering the Christian mission.

Illustrations

One of the clearest and earliest examples of this in the LEEO experience came through the presence of Muslims. I had previously worked only with Christians; indeed, for the most part only with Roman Catholics in residential treatment centers and a Catholic college for women. In these settings a common religious language and familiar religious practices were taken for granted as an integral part of the ministry.

LEEO presented a different situation. Several of the first participants were faithful members of the Muslim religion. They had their own religious language and religious customs. The challenge was to create an environment in which both the Christian and Muslim traditions could be affirmed. The key in meeting this challenge was to find a unifying principle which both could affirm with integrity. The way to do this was to attend carefully to how the Muslim brothers and sisters expressed their beliefs.

When this was done, two points became clear. The Muslim participants had a deep conviction about the supremacy and power of Allah. Every aspect of creation occurred with Allah's awareness. This belief generated a sense of trust and purpose in life. At the same time, this very belief instilled a desire and spirit of confidence in the individual to achieve the fulfillment of one's own potential. These values could be correlated with Christian belief in the sovereignty of God and the lordship of Jesus, which also generate a desire in the believer to fulfill oneself by doing God's will.

This correlation did not mean that Christianity and Islam were considered to be identical or that these beliefs exhausted the full meaning of either tradition. It simply meant that a caring environment was created which reflected the existing religious pluralism in the societal environment. This congruence made caring for society more effective because the persons cared for and those caring could affirm their respective identities with integrity.

This was both symbolized and promoted when a Muslim was hired as a supervisor of LEEO participants after they were employed. He was not hired because he was a Muslim, but the environment created in the program allowed him to express his beliefs freely. This enriched the overall atmosphere at LEEO, increased the awareness of other staff and program participants, and reinforced the feeling of acceptance experienced by new LEEO participants who were also Muslim.

A more difficult challenge was posed by linkages with persons or structures which were not religious. Whenever this occurs, it may be more difficult to affirm a Christian (or other religious) identity explictly. Indeed the value of doing so may even be subordinated to the goal of caring for society. In this case the quality of the care should serve as the affirmation of one's religious identity.

This challenge occurred in the LEEO experience when the original funding provided by the Lutheran church was running out. Explicit religious sources could not be identified to meet the growing budget. The only funding source that seemed adequate was the government, but to move in this direction caused discomfort for many who had initiated and supported LEEO as a church project.

How could this service still be called a Christian ministry if it was funded by the government? Would not government objectives and policies restrict LEEO, possibly even inject conflicts into its original motivation? These were real concerns. LEEO could not use the same religious language (e.g., missionary) and context (the gospel of Jesus) in submitting funding proposals to the government which it had used in stating its Articles of Incorporation. It had to translate ministerial references into government terminology. For example, concern for unemployed ex-offenders as an extension of the works of mercy became "employability assessment" and the community spirit of the staff became job descriptions within management by objectives.

But these shifts did not compromise what LEEO stood for or, more important, what it was able to accomplish. Precisely because of the government's funding (which necessitated a subordinating of LEEO's preferred religious language), LEEO was able to help ex-felons find jobs uninterruptedly for five more years. In addition, this challenge gave LEEO a fresh opportunity to assess its priorities, to determine its real motivation, to find ways to care for a pluralistic society with integrity. In the process, nothing essential was lost. No one who became acquainted with LEEO while it was under government funding ever thought this was "just another government program." They may not have known exactly what made it different, but they knew there was something different. And that something was the integrity of the program functioning as a Christian service in the midst of a pluralistic society.

What does this experience in the LEEO story have to say in general about caring for society? It says that caring for a pluralistic society will call for adaptations but should never call for the compromise of one's integrity. This is a great challenge which carries with it the opportunity to find new ways to affirm one's identity and to discover the real priorities of the service.

New Testament Reflections

This lesson is not entirely new, of course. Adaptation, reformulation, accommodation (or enculturation, as it is frequently called today) have been a constant feature of Christian service, beginning with Jesus himself. In fact, Jesus' ministry may be viewed in large part as an adaptation or reformulation of his own Judaism. At any rate, Jesus certainly evidenced this spirit in his teaching. His distinctive use of parables was intended to lead his hearers into a deeper experience of his message and of themselves. He did this by using stories and images which were part of everyday life. As the author of Mark's gospel comments, "By means of many such parables he taught them the message in a way they could understand" (Mark 4:33).

At other times his teaching reformulated and reinterpreted the existing understanding of religious value in Jewish life. The famous sermon on the mount (Matt. 5–7) is one collection of Jesus' interpretations, many of them quite distinctive: not only is murder liable to judgment but also anger; not only is adultery wrong but also lust; love is shown not only to friends but also to enemies. In all of this Jesus maintained, "Do not think that I have come to abolish the law and the prophets. I have come not to abolish them but to fulfill them" (Matt. 5:17).

Jesus did more than teach. He enacted his teaching—and it got him into trouble. On numerous occasions he adapted the existing Sabbath laws and other ritual norms to the needs of the situation. On one such occasion, recorded in Matthew 12:1-8, Jesus and his disciples were walking through the fields and eating the heads of grain. When they were challenged for breaking the Sabbath laws, Jesus responded by citing a higher value (and some precedents from Jewish history as well): "I assure you, there is something greater than the Temple here."

That "something greater" was what guided Jesus' adaptations and reformulations. It is the same principle which guides the flexibility of ministry at all times. Of course, Jesus did not minister in the kind of pluralistic society existing today. He could assume a shared religious worldview among his hearers. Within that common context he made adaptations.

It is a much more demanding and difficult challenge to exercise the same spirit of flexibility and to preserve one's integrity in a pluralistic environment. Living in a pluralistic society makes it more difficult to tell when a particular adaptation preserves the integrity of the ministry and when it compromises that integrity. This challenge has probably not been faced to the same degree since the time of St. Paul and the first adaptations of the Jewish-Christian message to the Greek-Gentile society.

The creative efforts of Paul's mission to the Gentiles often caused tension and misunderstanding with the Jewish Christians. On one occasion (Acts 21:15-26) when Paul was visiting Jerusalem, he was told that a number of Jewish Christians had heard that he was encouraging Jewish Christians who lived in Gentile areas (the diaspora) to abandon the Mosaic Law. Paul was teaching no such thing and to show his respect for the Mosaic Law, he agreed to accompany four Jewish Christians to the temple and pay the ritual fees for a vow they had taken. This accommodation was consistent with the integrity of Paul's ministry and the situation he was in, so he freely complied.

Not so consistent, in Paul's view, was an accommodation which Peter made. As Paul describes it in Galatians 2:11-14, Peter had been joining Gentile Christians for their agape (love) meals until some Jewish Christians began to object. Peter and other Jewish Christians then ceased their meal sharing, giving the impression that Gentile and Jewish Christians were really separate and should not eat together. Paul publicly confronted Peter and the others on this point, claiming that "they were not being straightforward about the truth of the gospel."

Part of the challenge of caring for a pluralistic society is constantly to evaluate whether particular adaptations enable the ministry to occur as fully as it can in a specific situation. Often it feels safer to rely on what is known and established. But in maintaining such safety, caring may be diminished.

It is not possible, of course, to set up criteria to govern every situation or to make error-free decisions. To care for society is risky, easily misunderstood, and often opposed. Today's pluralistic society doesn't make it any easier. Perhaps the most helpful lesson to be gleaned from the LEEO experience and from biblical reflection is that to care for society in a pluralistic environment means that the quality of caring is the primary affirmation of one's identity. A criterion accompanying this lesson is that in order to care for a pluralistic society, one should be regularly adapting, accommodating, and reformulating precisely in order to preserve the quality of caring for society.

2. RESISTANCE

Sometimes efforts to care for society are resisted. Certain attitudes, like racism, sexism, elitism, become so ingrained in the societal environment that they block effective service. These attitudes are not disembodied, of course. They are incarnate in individual persons, although they also do seem to have a life of their own. Resistance to caring service can be found anywhere in the societal environment as it comes to explicit expression in individual persons, on specific occasions.

The challenge when confronted by such resistance is twofold: (1) to maintain a clear, unmistakable stance on behalf of those who are being cared for, and (2) to do so without completely alienating the resisters or getting drawn into a distracting conflict with their resistant attitude. The crucial task is to care for others rather than defend oneself.

This is difficult to do because resistance to one's efforts is easily interpreted as resistance to oneself. Resistance calls into question, devalues, opposes what one feels committed to do for others. The instinctive reaction is to defend the choices one has made, to debate the resisters, to champion the validity of caring as one does.

A resistant attitude does call for response but the response must never detract from the work of caring for society. That is, defense of one's caring in and of itself should not replace the acts of caring. As noted in the previous section, these acts themselves are the best justification, not a theoretical argument which takes time and energy away from those to be cared for.

Illustrations

This principle had to be invoked in the LEEO experience on those (rather rare) occasions when a prospective employer would evidence a resistant, closed attitude about employing an ex-offender. The resistance did not come from an ignorance about the supportive services and incentives which LEEO offered to employers—tax credits, bonding, supervision of employees. These were always carefully explained ahead of time so an employer would know the program was well organized and sensitive to the risks and difficulties involved in hiring an ex-offender.

Nor did the resistance come from an ignorance about the extreme difficulties ex-offenders faced when seeking employment—the stigma of a prison record which remained even after a person had completed sentence, the lack of work experience and associated work habits, the stereotype of all ex-offenders as liable at any moment to commit the most heinous crime even if the original offense had been nonviolent. All these perceptions could usually be cleared up in a professional, responsible conversation.

No, the resistance that threatened to distract from the caring service was really a refusal to be willing to help. There was no strict reason for the refusal, only a strong emotional block that defied the LEEO representative to break through. In that instance, a game of competition was set up. The focus shifted from how an employer and a LEEO representative together could care for society to whether the LEEO representative could overcome an employer in a contest of resistance.

Whenever this attitude appeared, the standard practice by LEEO personnel was to close the conversation respectfully, gently, and quickly. An employer may have just set up a wall of resistance and would suddenly find that there was no one on the other side to resist. The refusal to engage in a distracting, self-serving debate was always accompanied by a sincere expression of appreciation for the time the employer had given and the hope that perhaps in the future some cooperation might be possible. More than once, a second meeting did occur and the resistant attitude seemed to give way to a more open one—leading occasionally to a hiring.

This was not always the case, of course, nor did the resistance come only from employers in the world of work. The resistance also came at times from groups of professed Christians. Certainly the most stinging example of this occurred during a critical period when funding for LEEO was in jeopardy. One of the members of LEEO's Board of Directors was able to use his professional position to convene a luncheon of influential Christian ministers. He invited me to describe the work of hiring ex-offenders as a ministry, deserving of financial support. The hope was that these Christian leaders would then solicit funding from their congregations to keep the program going.

I emphasized how good it was to speak the common language of Christian faith in this setting because so often (as indicated in the previous point) religious preferences had to be subordinated in order for LEEO to get the job done in a pluralistic society. After my presentation, the ministers reacted. Several of them pulled small Bibles from their vest pockets and began to quote sections of the New Testament in which they categorically excluded ex-offenders from the Kingdom of God. In committing crimes, these felons had chosen evil over good—as Satan had done. Jesus demanded faith in him in order to enter heaven; what did these ex-offenders believe in?

The resistance kept mounting. It quickly filled the room and canceled every attempt to respond. There was a refusal to be open that could only be likened to the hardening of hearts exposed so often in the very Bibles the ministers were quoting from. Their reaction was shocking because it was so unexpected, but it served to drive home the point that resistance to caring for society can appear anywhere in the societal environment.

What does this experience in the LEEO story have to say in general about caring for society? It says that caring for society at times confronts a spirit of resistance which offers the tempting invitation to leave the caring aside for a while and try to break down the resistance. The lesson from LEEO is that this is a seductive option which wastes time and energy. Such resistance is in fact an invitation to move on.

New Testament Reflections

Jesus taught the same lesson to his disciples. For example, in Luke 10:1-11 when he was preparing them for their ventures into the villages along his path to Jerusalem, he urged them to greet the residents with peace and to care for them. This care was expressed in terms of curing the sick who were in the town and announcing the reign of God to them. God's reign was the primary symbol which Jesus used to point to the presence of God's care and God's way of life as manifested in good effects—like curing illnesses. The assumption behind Jesus' advice was that people would respond favorably to this proclamation.

However, "if the people of any town you enter do not welcome you, go into its streets and say, 'We shake the dust of this town from our feet as testimony against you. But know that the reign of God is near'" (vv. 10-11).

The setting for these instructions was most likely charged with a sense of urgency that time was running out before the climactic events of Jesus' ministry and his own confrontation with the resistance he faced in his environment. However Jesus or his disciples envisioned that climax, it seemed to provoke an urgency that is not usually felt in our societal environment today (except perhaps when we are confronted by the prospect of nuclear destruction).

This does not mean that those who care for society do not feel urgent about their task, but it does mean that they assume society will still be here tomorrow. From a Christian viewpoint the final confrontation between good and evil has already taken place. Every subsequent occasion reenacts that event, but it *is not* that event; that event has been completed once and for all in Jesus' ministry. Other religions view the contest between good and evil in their own way, but usually they offer some basis for hoping in the victory of good over evil. Different ways of responding to resistance would follow from these different interpretations. In any event, there was a unique urgency in Jesus' exhortation to his disciples. The uniqueness has passed but not the urgency (1 Pet. 3:13-17).

Similarly, the symbol of shaking the dust from one's feet is a more final, counterresistance than the open-ended response which LEEO customarily gave when it faced resistance. Here again, the modern assumption is that every occasion, even one filled with resistance, opens onto other occasions. To take an adamant stance in the present is to foreclose possibilities in the future. The challenge is to take a clear, unmistakable stance while not closing off those future possibilities.

The first Christians faced this challenge often. The advice found in 1 Peter 3:13-17 was typical then and relevant now. When confronted with resistance, even persecution and suffering, Christians were reminded, "Who indeed can harm you if you are committed deeply to doing what is right?" This might be paraphrased, If you are deeply committed to caring for society, why spend time defending yourself against those who resist your efforts?

Further, "Should anyone ask you the reason for this hope of yours, be ever ready to reply, but speak gently and respectfully." The spirit of this advice seems to be, respond if there is opportunity and do so in a way that opens up the best possibility for change in others and increased caring for society. That was certainly LEEO's experience and the lesson that emerges from that experience is that caring for society is too important to get sidetracked with no-win confrontations. A criterion that accompanies this lesson is that to care for society with appropriate urgency, one should periodically shake the dust from one's feet but always gently and respectfully so that when and if resistant persons are ready to share in a caring service, the environment is open, receptive, and appreciative.

3. PUBLICNESS

Caring for society is a public activity. The alternative to a public, caring service is a privatized form of care which does not nurture the public life of society adequately. Caring for society directs attention and energy to those persons and structures which are in need of service, but it is just one of the numerous activities which comprise societal life. And because society is so pluralistic, so diversified, so active, a caring service inevitably competes for the attention and resources it needs to be effective.

A pivotal role in this regard is played by the media of public information and persuasion, especially television, radio, and newspapers. The prime challenge is twofold: (1) to utilize the media to proclaim that our society is worth caring for and is in fact being cared for in certain specific instances, and (2) to do so in a way that affirms the integrity of the media and their own purposes. When this is done effectively, the potential of the media to help care for society is also actualized. This in itself is an exercise in caring for society although it is secondary to the primary intention of caring.

When the media are used to tell a story, to make an appeal, to affirm a value, they function as a means to an end. In this instance the media are not the ministry but they contribute to the ministry by opening larger segments of the society to the fact (and sometimes the experience) of people and places in society which need caring for.

A balance must be struck, however. The end result of media exposure must be to advance the prospects of caring for society more adequately. If attention turns to those who do the caring or if those who are cared for are exploited for sensationalist or curiosity purposes, then the public character of caring for society has been misplaced and the caring has been compromised.

Illustrations

This was a constant tension in publicizing LEEO. Publicity was sought in order to find additional jobs, to raise needed income, and to educate the public about ex-offenders who were really trying to change their lives. Reporters ordinarily were not interested in merely describing a service program like LEEO. They needed an angle, a story, an event that would catch the attention of their audience and gain favorable reaction to the medium for presenting it—even if the story itself was unpleasant or disquieting.

In the case of LEEO the basic story ran counter to prevailing societal attitudes. Why should people appreciate efforts to find jobs for ex-offenders when so many law-abiding citizens were out of work and no one was helping them find jobs? Why should special efforts be made to help people who had harmed society (and who, according to recidivism statistics as well as the popular stereotype, would likely do so again)? The caring answer is, of course, that the greatest effort should go to those with the greatest need. Care is not a reward for good behavior but a response to deficiencies that prevent people from realizing their fulfillment.

This answer, however, is not news. It does not warrant inclusion in the media's selection of stories. The fact that a Roman Catholic sister was directing the LEEO program and working in the secular arena of government, business, and the courts had some media appeal, but that was precisely the misplaced emphasis that had to be avoided. Highlighting a curiosity angle would not further the care of society.

The key to propagating the public character of LEEO's work was to lead the reporter into LEEO's story at a point which satisfied the media's need for news and simultaneously expressed the core of the caring service. (This is the same approach, described above, that was used to meet the challenge of pluralism.) The contact point was not always obvious and often demanded that the focus of the caring dimension shift (also similar to the response to pluralism).

This occurred most clearly in the case of one ex-offender, Robert James, whose story was told in chapter four. Robert had been working productively on a job he secured through LEEO and then was fired after a routine spot-check showed that he had been convicted of a felony. When informed of this development, a reporter became incensed at the injustice caused by a bureaucratic policy. This was not the primary concern of LEEO but it was integrally connected to it and led to a story which helped change the policy.

Even when a reporter found an angle worth reporting, there were some further, peculiar problems involved. Several companies had agreed to hire ex-offenders from the LEEO program but had done so without publicizing that fact. Sometimes this was to avoid negative reactions from customers; sometimes it was to avoid unfair pressure on the ex-offender from peer workers. Either reason made it more difficult to publicize the facts of LEEO's success.

Here, too, individuals in the media were very cooperative. In filming TV stories, for example, the camera would not show the ex-offenders directly. In referring to companies which had hired them, the reporter would just describe the type of business without naming the company. On one occasion, a reporter's story was ready to go to print when it was learned that the family of the ex-offender did not want his name used. At the very last minute, the reporter substituted a fictitious name.

These accommodations were not trivial matters. It was hard for reporters not to include all the facts and details available. Part of the reason for their spirit of cooperation was the reporters' experience of what LEEO actually meant. They met the ex-offenders; they saw their efforts to change and overcome societal opposition; they witnessed the support and dedication of the LEEO staff in trying to help the participants. In short, they became part of the occasions they reported. They did not cease to be reporters, to ask journalistic questions, or to push for an angle that would be newsworthy. But they could do their job with integrity while being drawn into the job LEEO was doing, also with integrity.

Another forum for proclaiming the care of society is public hearings. These are usually related to legislative procedures and are decidedly political. Nonetheless, the purpose of public hearings is to gather the experience and wisdom of the community on issues of societal importance. They are an opportunity to enhance the public character of caring.

LEEO had this opportunity twice regarding national legislation: on March 2, 1984, before the U.S. Senate Subcommittee on Economic Growth, Employment, and Revenue Sharing and again on April 16, 1984, before the House Subcommittee on Select Revenue Measures. Both the Senate and House subcommittees were considering a recommendation to renew existing legislation which would give a tax credit to employers who hired people considered hard to employ. The legislation, Targeted Jobs Tax Credit (TJTC), had included ex-offenders and was one of the incentives LEEO used in approaching prospective employers.

Because of LEEO's extensive and successful experience with the TJTC for ex-offenders, I was invited to prepare written testimony which would go into the Congressional Record and to speak for three minutes as well as answer questions from the subcommittee. Although this was a brief exposure and it served larger legislative purposes, it nonetheless provided an occasion for affirming the public character of LEEO's service and for acquainting others with what could be done to help care for society. No attempt was made to overstate the experience of LEEO or to make unfounded claims or accusations. Rather the value and benefits of caring in this way stood on their own merits and were proclaimed as such.

What does this experience in the LEEO story have to say in general about caring for society? It says that caring for society in a public way calls for reliance on the intrinsic value of the caring service. This means that a great deal of confidence is invested in the genuineness of the care which is given and in the openness of media personnel to respond to that genuineness, albeit in their terms and from their own interests.

This means further that one must be able to recognize the witness value in caring for society when it is expressed in different forms. This stands in sharp contrast to orchestrating attention-getting events for the sake of "coverage." Caring for society goes deeper than that. It also requires more—a consistent, sincere commitment to care for others first, and to leave public attention in the hands of media professionals. As a result, one does not completely control the public image which is given to one's work.

New Testament Reflections

This fact is sometimes troublesome, as Jesus' disciples found. Once, when they were proclaiming their message and working their caring service, they noticed someone who was not of their group saying and doing the same kind of thing. When they presented this problem to Jesus, he reversed it and invoked the principle "anyone who is not against us is with us" (Mark 9:38-41). In one sense this is the lesson LEEO learned about the media and the public character of caring. More than that, LEEO learned that many were indeed with them not by default (i.e., because they were not against them) but by conscious choice.

At the same time, the disciples of Jesus also found themselves on (at least) one occasion unable to perform the caring service which others needed and which they wanted to give. As the story is told in Matthew 17:14-21, a man brought his son to the disciples. The son had suffered from seizures since childhood and would throw himself into fire or water. The disciples could not cure him, but Jesus did. When the disciples asked him why they could not help, he told them bluntly, "because you have so little trust." Further, their trust was undernourished because they did not pray and fast sufficiently, that is, they were not in union with the source of all genuine caring.

The lesson from this incident, and from the preceding one as well, is that to care for others, one's motives must be constantly purified. To pray and fast is a biblical way of saying that care for others is what motivates one's action, not publicity, not gratification, not imitation or repetition of previous successful activity. The demands of caring are always prior to observable effects. Unless those demands are met (sometimes by actual prayer and fasting), no observable effects ought to result or be publicized.

This lesson about the public character of caring appears often in the life of St. Paul, but perhaps nowhere as clearly as in the incidents reported in Acts 21-26. Paul's conflicts with the Jewish Christians were described earlier (in regard to pluralism). His conflicts with Jews who did not become Christians were worse. They saw Paul as a threat because they cared so deeply about their traditional religion, which he seemed to be undermining. Throughout, Paul invoked every means at his disposal to get a hearing for his message. In particular he appealed to his rights as a Roman citizen (Acts 22:25-29) in order to speak publicly and frequently (Acts 24–26).

In doing so, Paul was being more than a little manipulative, using the legal system of his day to serve his own purposes. But at the same time he was calling upon the legal system to function as the legal system was supposed to. In fulfilling its stated purpose, it was also serving his purpose.

LEEO learned that it isn't necessary to manipulate the media or political processes to enhance the public character of caring, but it is desirable to offer them opportunities both to fulfill their own purpose and at the same time to bear witness to the care of society. The lesson to be taken from LEEO and New Testament reflection is that the first responsibility is to care, genuinely and confidently, and only after that to publicize. The criterion that accompanies this lesson is that from time to time some other people should get the public credit for one's own care of society and they will describe that care in their own (nonreligious) way. When that happens, the proper response should be satisfaction, for if they are not against, they are for.

4. IDENTIFICATION

In a pluralistic, complex, and competitive society, it is important for people who need care to identify those who can give care. One of the goals of publicity and one of the motives for attending to the public character of caring service is to let people know where they can locate the care they need. If contact cannot be made, care often cannot be given.

Along with location, definition is important. Caring does not occur in general, even if its scope is all of society. Caring occurs in definable, limited episodes. These concrete occasions serve specific aims which give them definition. Being located somewhere and having defined aims need not restrict the caring to just this one place and these limited goals. Rather, location and definition form the concrete base from which caring reaches out beyond its own context.

This means that caring is not limited only to direct delivery of services. If that were the case, it would be hard to speak intelligently of the care of society. Although all caring is rooted somewhere and aims at specific goals, its efforts can reach far beyond the confines of a particular place or purpose. On the other hand, unless it is rooted somewhere, caring can turn into a broad appeal with no grounding in concrete reality.

Illustrations

These points were part of the LEEO experience from the very beginning. The program had been established to find jobs for women and men who had already been released from prison rather than for those still incarcerated. This definition of the role of LEEO was necessary because participants had to be available to go on job interviews and begin work immediately if they were hired. At the same time, it was essential that LEEO be located in a reachable spot so that participants, who usually had no private means of transportation, could get back and forth conveniently.

It wasn't long before men and women who were still incarcerated began to write to LEEO. (The value of their letters is described more fully in chapter eight.) With the very first letter it was clear that LEEO had been located. In addition, their communication connected two very concretely defined places. The inmates, like anyone confined to a given space, yearned for contact with the larger world. Just as a visitor provides that contact, bringing human presence and an experience of caring, so too LEEO became a kind of visitor (without leaving its location or changing its purpose).

Simply knowing that a program like LEEO actually existed, had a mailing address, included some real, caring persons was a great sign of hope to those incarcerated women and men who learned of its existence. For so many of them, the corrections system seemed to toy with their future. They may have been declared eligible for parole if they could secure employment or show in their parole plan that a job awaited them upon release. But, of course, it was virtually impossible to find employment while still incarcerated. The prospect of freedom offered on the one hand seemed to be snatched away by the provisions held in the other hand of the criminal justice system.

Even those who were incarcerated in distant prisons like those in California, Texas, and Kansas felt that their hope was more tangible if they could write to LEEO. And their hope was reinforced when they would receive a letter in reply, describing LEEO's services and the procedure for entering the program. Every inmate who contacted LEEO was sent a response. The response may not have been a solution for their particular case, but it confirmed them in knowing where care could be found.

In addition to the inmates whom LEEO could not help directly and the program participants whom it could help, there were others in the extended relationship of LEEO's caring. These included an ex-offender's heartbroken mother who could now take pride in her son's accomplishments on a job site; a participant's wife who had spent years faithfully waiting for the day of his release; a female participant's child who now had a role model who was employed, who provided for the needs of her family, and who could speak credibly about the importance of getting a good education and making a success of life.

Service to the family and friends of LEEO participants was not part of the program's definition, but that never prevented good effects from spreading out to a larger community of individuals. They in turn may never have visited the actual offices of LEEO but they knew such a program existed in fact and not just in someone's good intentions or on an unfunded proposal form. By having a definite location and a defined purpose, LEEO was not restricted in its caring for society but was enabled to care clearly, effectively, and expansively.

What does this experience in the LEEO story have to say in general about caring for society? It says that to care for society it is necessary to be identifiable, and identification is rooted primarily in a clear definition of the service to be offered. Location follows from definition. It is not necessary to do the same service all the time or to be in the same place all the time, but it is necessary for others to know what services are available and where they can be found. In fact, if the caring service is relevant to people's real needs, they will usually manage to locate it.

New Testament Reflections

This, in any event, was true in Jesus' ministry. He moved around so much that when one person expressed a desire to follow him, he had to say that "the foxes have lairs, the birds in the sky have nests, but the Son of Man has nowhere to lay his head" (Matt. 8:19-20). A mobile ministry has its price and not everyone is prepared to pay it. But despite the personal inconvenience and fluidity of Jesus' ministry, people knew how to find him.

On several occasions when Jesus and his disciples tried to get away for a little privacy, they couldn't. As noted in Mark 6:30-33, "people saw them leaving and many got to know about it. People from all the towns hastened on foot to the place, arriving ahead of them." Of course, Jesus moved within a relatively small geographic area and in the midst of a stable society where people's whereabouts were more easily known than today. Nonetheless, effective ministry has a way of being located. This is not to say that an address and phone number and business cards are not needed; it is to say that they are not a replacement for the primacy of caring service.

In addition to finding Jesus, people undoubtedly had mixed motives for wanting to be around him. Their reasons for finding him were not always his reasons. Often people were just curious, looking for signs or marvels that he might work (Matt. 12:38; 16:1-4). At other times they just wanted to argue about his religious interpretations; they didn't want to go beyond the debate to make decisions and changes in their lives (Luke 10:25-37; John 3; 12:42).

One notable exception was Zaccheus, whose story is told in Luke 19:1-10. As a tax collector, Zaccheus was on the fringe of Jewish social life; as a short man, he couldn't see over the crowd when Jesus came by. Zaccheus overcame both disadvantages by climbing a sycamore tree and satisfying his curiosity to see Jesus. But when Jesus offered him a deeper experience, Zaccheus accepted and changed his life, promising to give half his belongings to the poor and paying back fourfold anyone he had defrauded (which may have been everyone he ever collected taxes from).

The response of Zaccheus was consistent with the purpose of Jesus' ministry—to proclaim the presence of God's reign and to invite appropriate change (liberation) in people's lives. This purpose defined Jesus' ministry; it clarified what he would and would not do. He consistently avoided, for example, any attempt to make him the leader of a mass political movement (John 7) or to accept him only as a healer and wonder worker (John 12:9).

At the same time, Jesus' understanding of the limits of his ministry could be altered. At the wedding feast of Cana when the wine ran out, Jesus at first indicated that it was not time for him to begin his public ministry. "My hour has not yet come." And yet, at his mother's prompting, he acted on behalf of the wedding couple (John 2:1-11).

On another occasion, when he was approached by a Canaanite woman to help her sick daughter, he responded rather curtly, "My mission is only to the lost sheep of the house of Israel." When she persisted with a sincerity and cleverness that typified what the house of Israel should be, Jesus responded positively to her request (Mark 7:24-30). Both of these instances show Jesus reshaping the limits of his defined purpose without abandoning that purpose. They also suggest the persuasive power of women in the story of salvation. The same spirit characterized St. Paul's defined mission of preaching to the Gentiles rather than to the Jews. He never wavered from that commitment although he kept reshaping its specific form and limits, as already noted in the way he related to Jewish Christians.

The lesson which emerges from these New Testament references and from reflection on LEEO's story is that caring for society is most effective when its purpose is clearly defined. Moreover, such definition helps to locate where that caring can be found or should be situated. In addition, a defined purpose is not restrictive or inhibiting. It actually facilitates effective caring because it provides a definite base to operate from and a framework within which to reshape the actual services given. A criterion which accompanies this lesson is that to care well for society, some services should not be offered and those which are, should periodically get reshaped and redefined.

5. LINKAGES

To care effectively for society, one cannot work alone. As noted in the discussion on pluralism, it is necessary to form linkages with others, to avoid duplication of services, and to identify appropriate ways in which people can be of help. The assumption underlying any effort to care for society is that people do want to be of assistance and they will indicate in what ways and to what extent they can join in.

The crucial value here is timing, and the chief challenge is to identify accurately what type of support a person is willing to give. Sometimes a person or organization is prepared to lend a type of support that is premature or marginal to the defined purposes of the program. In the LEEO experience this occurred from time to time when volunteer groups wanted to know what they could do to help. In fact, there was very little they could do as volunteers to assist the program directly. The specific services of LEEO required professional, full-time workers—unlike a prison visitation ministry or a public educational effort which might depend primarily on volunteers. Moreover, I had prior experience conducting an all-volunteer literacy aid program and knew the necessity of organizing, supporting, and reinforcing volunteers. To do this well would take away from the primary purpose of LEEO (finding jobs) or require additional staff for which there was no money. Out of respect for the volunteers, LEEO declined their help.

It is never easy to turn down an offer to help; but that may be the most effective (and honest) response to give, accompanied, of course,

ments or to call in to the program and explain their absence. Program participants who missed three scheduled contacts with LEEO without having called the office were advised that they were terminated from the program. In this way, these participants understood that they were not sufficiently job ready.

These strict expectations were not intended to dominate people or put them under undue pressure. They were meant to say that LEEO took its participants seriously and could not offer them its service adequately unless there was a consistent, mutual commitment. Freedom did not mean showing up whenever a person felt like it, but showing up in order to allow the program to be of help.

Not everyone responded appropriately even after securing a job. Marlene, for example, had received all the job-related services offered through LEEO. She had been subsequently hired by the personnel director of a large hotel. In addition, the hotel personnel division provided Marlene with training as a word processor and offered her excellent chances for upward mobility. Despite all these advantages, Marlene began to exhibit behaviors that led to her dismissal.

Nothing disappointed the LEEO staff more than this kind of news. It was hard to understand why a person who had received extensive services and support could let it all go. At such times, it was essential to recall the guiding word in the program's very name, liberation. Every participant was free and the services of LEEO were freely offered.

In cases like Marlene's, persons were usually told that their behaviors indicated that LEEO was not the program for them. Their own freedom and integrity were left intact. If a judgment was being made, it was a judgment on the limitations of LEEO as it was structured.

At the same time, it was always hard to measure the full success of LEEO. If freedom was prized as the primary goal, then some persons may have been acting most freely (for them) when they chose to leave LEEO. They may have learned through LEEO that they did have choices and that every choice had both positive and negative consequences. For several participants who had been "broken" during their prison terms and had become very passive, docile persons, a deliberate choice to leave LEEO was a sign of success even though no job had been found for the person.

The same characteristic of freedom applied to the staff itself. The freedom expected of the participants had to be modeled by the staff. This meant that a climate had to be created in which each staff person felt free to do what was expected, to determine the degree of personal investment in doing the job as a caring service, and to be trusted to use their full potential in everything they did.

The risks, the challenges, and the difficulties in measuring success all make freedom a volatile value. But LEEO accepted the challenge because at the heart of its service were persons and both the caring persons and those cared for were meant to be free.

What does this experience in the LEEO story have to say in general about caring for society? It says that caring persons must prize everyone's freedom to make choices within a structured pursuit of goals. Without structure, freedom is license and not very helpful in achieving growth. Without freedom, structure is oppressive and not very caring.

New Testament Reflections

Jesus knew this. He always respected the freedom of others to make their own choices. One of the clearest examples of this is recorded in John's gospel (6:25-71). After he had fed the multitude (John 6:1-15), Jesus began to apply his action to himself, claiming to be the bread of life which enables others to live forever if they eat of it. Many of his followers remarked, "This sort of talk is hard to endure. How can anyone take it seriously?"

Jesus persisted in his teaching and "many of his disciples broke away and would not remain in his company any longer." Jesus did not run after them, but turned to his most trusted friends, the twelve, and asked, "Do you want to leave me too?" He gave people their freedom—even his betrayer, as the gospel notes in concluding this story (vv. 70-71).

None of Jesus' followers proclaimed the value of freedom more consistently or boldly than did Paul. His conviction is expressed succinctly in Galatians 5:1. "It was for liberty that Christ freed us." Paul constantly urged, chided, begged his hearers not to return to former ways, which were in fact dependent on some other norm of life. But he also did not want his affirmation of freedom to be misinterpreted. "Remember that you have been called to live in freedom—but not a freedom that gives free rein to the flesh" (Gal. 5:13). Freedom is not license; it is the structure and spirit of a caring life.

The lesson which emerges from these New Testament references and from general reflection on the LEEO story is that caring persons respect the freedom of each person. That freedom is strengthened when it is experienced in a structure that is clearly explained and consistently followed. A criterion that accompanies this lesson is that success in caring for society should be measured by how freely people do what they do, not by how completely they fulfill a caring person's expectations.

5. CREATIVE

Caring is an art that draws from previous experience in order to respond as effectively as possible to present needs and possibilities. In doing so, caring persons seek to be creative rather than repetitious. Often the creative dimension of caring focuses on the selection and use of the means to achieve a particular purpose. When other persons are engaged in this way, creative caring can open up new possibilities for them as well.

Illustrations

One example of this in the LEEO experience pertained to job readiness training. Such a key element in the process of finding jobs for ex-offenders demanded the most creative approach. Skilled staff members developed a number of exercises and practical sessions on what to expect, how to prepare a resumé and fill out an application form, the importance of a good appearance, etc., but these were still one step removed from the actual experience.

When the LEEO staff faced this challenge creatively, two possibilities opened up. One was to seek the use of video equipment to tape practice job interviews; the other was to solicit the help of those in personnel work to conduct practice job interviews.

The District Court Office of Federal Probation had already been screening and referring ex-offenders to LEEO. When one of their staff members was approached about the idea of videotaping practice job interviews, he agreed to arrange for LEEO to use their video equipment free of charge on a biweekly basis. This contribution made a tremendous difference in job readiness because now LEEO participants could see and hear how they presented themselves. This made them more willing and better able to improve their presence, eye contact, speaking voice, etc.

At the same time, personnel representatives from several area businesses expressed a willingness to conduct practice job interviews on videotape and share in the feedback-critique sessions afterwards. On some occasions the practices turned into on-the-spot job offers when the interviewer realized the potential of the person being interviewed.

In both of these instances persons who were already engaged in their own professional work were invited to pursue new possibilities which were integral to their work and helpful to LEEO as well. Caring persons who are creative in finding the means to meet their goals can often tap the creative, caring capacity in others.

Sometimes this can happen with someone who is already using a professional position in a caring way. One woman who was a staff member of a community rehabilitation program customarily brought used clothes and other donated items to her office. She made these available to clients whom she counseled. This generosity went beyond her strict job description and was indicative of her caring spirit.

LEEO provided her with an opportunity to do even more. Some persons who applied to LEEO did not have a parole or probation officer. The structure of the program required a referral source who would also screen the applicants. The woman mentioned above agreed to serve in this capacity. She saw in this service a chance to extend her own caring efforts while helping LEEO meet its needs in a creative way.

Creativity sometimes requires letting go of familiar and established ways of doing things. This can initially feel like a real loss, but new gains cannot occur until creative changes are put in place. When steps are taken creatively and in a caring way, new possibilities emerge and apparent loss turns to actual gain.

What does this experience in the LEEO story have to say in general about caring for society? It says that caring persons are challenged to be creative. Moreover, the exercise of their creativity can open up new possibilities for others while meeting the goals and objectives of their own caring service.

New Testament Reflections

Jesus did this often in his ministry. On one occasion, narrated in John 4:1-42, Jesus was resting at a well while his disciples had gone off to get some food. A Samaritan woman came by to draw water from the well. Jesus asked her for some water. With that, they began a conversation which not only changed the woman's life but prompted her to be a messenger to her townsfolk on behalf of Jesus.

In one sense, every time Jesus crossed anyone's path, he elicited from them new possibilities for their own living. This was certainly true of those he called to follow him, but it also applied to people like the paralyzed man whom he cured after forgiving his sins (Luke 5:17-26), the woman caught in adultery whom he saved from stoning and liberated by his acceptance of her (John 8:1-11), and even Pilate, the Roman official who condemned him to death, whom he touched in dialogue by speaking truthfully (John 18:28–19:16).

Jesus' disciples also took a creative approach to proclaiming the good news, especially as they tried to draw upon the experience and social position of others. Paul's appeal to Philemon, already cited in this chapter, is one example of this. So, too, is his attempt to get his Greek listeners in Athens to think in a creative way about their "unknown god" (Acts 17:16-34). They already held some respect for such a deity; Paul tried to lead them to his Lord and God through their own convictions.

The lesson which emerges from these New Testament references and from general reflection on the story of LEEO is that caring persons engage in a creative task which opens up new possibilities for others. A criterion which accompanies this lesson is that other people should discover new possibilities for themselves when they respond to one's invitation to care for society.

SUMMARY

In this chapter caring persons have been examined in light of the LEEO experience. In that experience caring persons are characterized as open to those cared for, surprising in the responses they give, spiritually powerful, free, and creative in their interactions with others.

Those cared for are a real source of caring service, and one can never predetermine who is and who is not willing to serve as a caring person. Power is rooted in the spirit of societal life and manifested primarily through those cared for. Freedom guides the interaction of all those who care for one another and for society, and creativity helps one to meet personal goals while opening new possibilities for others.

Out of this same experience come certain criteria which guide one's caring service. Such care should be traceable to actual experiences with those cared for; it should periodically ask the least likely persons to help; it should begin sometimes without all the resources securely in place; it should be judged by how free people are to act on their own choices; and it should mean that those who are asked for help discover new possibilities for themselves which they never realized before.

The five characteristics of the societal environment (chapter six) and the five characteristics of caring persons are united in a final lesson derived from the LEEO experience. Caring is activity. There is always a danger of postponing action until enough study and preparation have been done. Obviously, one should not move into action compulsively or naively. But a greater danger exists today that one's caring will be delayed until the groundwork is firmly and finally laid and all eventualities have been anticipated and provided for.

The experience of LEEO has been that action is what the Lord wants. This allows one to learn from experience, to respond to actual occasions, to stay in touch with the movement of the Lord in the lives of people and society. Caring for society is not just planning to care or analyzing completely the context of caring. It is caring. LEEO has learned that there is no better preparation.

PART FOUR

From Society to the Cell

THE LEEO PROGRAM was designed to find jobs for women and men after they had been released from prison. But this did not prevent those who were still incarcerated from contacting LEEO. Between 1977 and 1984 the LEEO program received hundreds of letters from men and women incarcerated in local jails, state institutions, and federal prisons throughout the United States.

In contrast to the previous sections of this book, the movement of this part is from society to the cell. This refers to the response which society can give to those women and men who are still incarcerated. LEEO tried to respond to them once they were released, but an equally critical challenge faces society as a whole in regard to prisoners before their release. That challenge is articulated in the words of the inmates themselves. A caring, effective response from society is yet to be heard. The following chapter intends to be the beginning of such a response.

First, the content of the letters which LEEO received from prisoners in thirty-seven states will be summarized. Excerpts from these letters are reprinted verbatim. Then a reflection on their meaning, including specific suggestions to help meet the needs expressed in the letters, will be offered. Finally, a faith reflection will conclude the chapter.

I'am a D.C resident I live with
my mother. I have two Kid I have a daughter she
IS 3 year old and my son IS 1 year old. I Need
a job badly I am trying to get released from
Cornt. I have a B.R.Q. Bail Reform Act.
I go back to Cornt Oct. 3, 1983 but I have Never
ben IN troble before. I have a young family
I Never ben IN A program. I No the only way I program
Can help If I be out on the street but If jugde
put me IN a program I hope to be IN this one
I do Need a job because I have responsibities

CHAPTER EIGHT

The Letters

AN ANALYSIS OF THE LETTERS LEEO received reveals a number of common characteristics among the inmates who wrote to the LEEO program. These characteristics do not necessarily apply to all prison inmates, but they do come from a rather large sampling and certainly typify the persons who contacted LEEO.

1. REQUEST FOR ASSISTANCE

While in prison, residents are separated from family and friends. They live in an environment that radically limits their personal freedom. This experience of isolation produces emotional and psychological needs which are rarely met adequately within the institution. Depending on the institution in which they are incarcerated, inmates may also be in need of medical or dental care. Most suffer from the effects of being in overcrowded prisons—a factor of growing concern throughout the U.S. today. The requests for assistance usually focused on employment opportunities and job-related needs. In many cases, the inmate's primary concern was for family members. An example of this appears on the previous page.

I received your letter, and I'm very happy to hear that you're interested in helping me with my present situation. I also received that letter that your friends wrote to my caseworker about coming out here to see me, and my caseworker said that he would have it approved so they could come to see me, right now I'm in a very small cell, and I'm only allowed to come out for an hour a day for a shower's, I'm suppose to be waiting to be transfered to Atlanta, but it seem's that its taking so long that I'm getting really depressed about it, if you could I'd appreciate it if you'd check into this for me.

Let me hear from you soon

2. FEELINGS OF DEPRESSION

For most inmates, life in prison is very dehumanizing and produces strong feelings of depression and worthlessness. Many institutions lack appropriate counseling, educational, training, and employment programs for those incarcerated. Residents often pass the time in idleness and are left to their slim resources to survive as best they can. A letter from one inmate summed up the mood accurately—and expressed his thanks in verse.

Thanks

Thank you for your Words of Care, you've helped to make my day, you've made me that I'm Not Far From home even though I'm miles away, No words Can stop the loneliness, but you've helped to ease the pain, you've made me believe in sunshine even though there's only rain, I've been sad most of my time here, but I know I shouldn't be, because the world is full of people who hurt much more than me, I'd gladly stay here Forever if it would Change the problems of the world, Bring peace to places Where there's war, and Food to every hungry boy and Girl.

3. EXPRESSION OF GRATITUDE

Because of the state of emotional and often physical deprivation in which the residents exist, most expressed a heightened sense of gratitude for any assistance they received. They would write letters to judges, lawyers, community-based organizations, and prospective employers. Few, if any, of these persons ever responded to the letters. Consequently, a letter from LEEO advising the residents of the conditions for being admitted into the program meant a great deal to them. One inmate expressed what so many others felt.

This is to certify that I have reviewed and acknowledg your reply from my last missive. "Words can't possibly utter the appreciation I feel at this time for your ex-offenders program assistance for me!

---

4. ABILITY TO HOPE

The intrinsic desire within all persons to continue living strengthens the ability of those incarcerated to continue hoping. Regardless of the length of prison sentence, the deplorable conditions of prison living, and the absence of any viable support system, their letters reflected a powerful expression of hope. Many of them based their hope on faith in God or a "supreme power." Examples of both follow.

But I hope by becoming a part of your meeting program, I would be able to be productive and responsible. As was mention in the first part of the letter I will be home in the next 90 days or sooner, if I get a bed in the half-way house, next month. I hope to hear from you concerning my letters and getting me employment where I can be useful, I am willing, for I would rather struggle trying to do that which is right, then die a stagnated life of imprisonment

---

I know God will keep his promise, and he will not allow me to be tested beyond my power to remain firm, at the time I am put to the test, he will give me the strength to endure it, and so provide me with a way out, I do hope you are able to help me find this way out and help me save the rest of my life

---

5. OPENNESS

The residents evidenced a striking openness in the disclosure of their past history and personal problems. They did not blame others for their situation. Rather, they revealed themselves through their letters sincerely, without the trappings of self-righteousness or a denial by self-pity. The following is an example.

I was parolled from the Attica Facility in January 1973 after serving a one to three year sentence for a 2nd degree forgery conviction. From that time I have been employed, self sufficient and free of trouble with the authorities for a period of ten years. Now I am about to be returned to my present home in Washington, D.C. where I have resided for over two years, and I will need all the assistance I am able to get to secure employment in the Washington area. I will require contacts in the District that will assist the ex-offender that is being returned to the community. With a depressed job market an ex-offender that is Black, 54 years of age, and without a personal job contact will undoubtedly find the going difficult to say the least. In what ever way you can assist me will be greatly appreciated.

I look forward to hearing from you.

---

6. EXPERIENCE OF CHANGE

Many of the residents who wrote to LEEO experienced a change in their lives. They understood the gravity of their offense committed against others in society. They longed to be different, in order to avoid repeating past behaviors. That realization was a major change—and a significant one, as expressed in this letter.

I thought I would write and ask you for an chance to prove to you and the Community, that given a Chance that I am and always was an responsible human being. whom made a mistake in my life because of lack of responsible efforts toward me on my part. I'm very Contrite and duly Compassionate what I have done that brought myself to this place of torment. But given a chance I can become what was always inside me and that is an responsible Citizen.

Thank you
Respectfully
Submitted.

---

7. DESIRE TO HELP OTHERS

Many residents expressed a desire to work in situations where they might help other persons. For example, those who had been convicted of drugs longed to work with young people in sports or recreation programs in order to advise them of the dangers of addiction. Many expressed an interest in assisting the handicapped, the elderly, or the ill. This interest in helping others may have been a self-imposed form of retribution, or an expression of a willingness to change, or a latent development in their socio-relational awareness. Whatever the cause, the effect was clearly expressed, as in this example.

---

the thought entered my mind that maybe I would be able to get some help from you, more importantly, that I would be able to offer you my help and, hopefully my presence and experience would serve as an example to other's, that if I'm able to pull myself out of this morass that I'm submerged in, through education, what the advantages could be if one did'nt have a prison record to overcome in order to compete in employment pursuit. That if I could dissuade one youngster from treading this road that would make it worthwhile. That just one would look at how much energy I have to expend to keep afloat and he/she would channel that energy into constructive thinking.

---

8. EMPLOYMENT

The need for employment is critical among those imprisoned because it is often the single most important factor in determining their release from the institution. Even though inmates have received parole, they frequently may not be released from prison unless they have secured a job. As one inmate wrote, "I've been paroled since Feb. 18, '83 but unable to be released because I don't have a job, it's been 7 months since my parole date, even a part-time job would set me free."

The letters indicated a level of awareness on the part of the residents with regard to their employability. They often enclosed resumés, discussed their past work experience or job qualifications, and identified the kinds of work they were interested in.

I'm presently 4 months away from completing a 1 to 3 yr. sentence, and due to the fact that; although I'm looking forward to being returned to the community on or around aug. 8th, 1983, I'll be in dying need of some aid and assistance as far as seeking and acquiring gainful employment. My problem in the area of getting gainful employment is truly many-fold—① first and foremost, I'm unskilled, ② I'm returning to the community labelled "ex-convict," and ③ I don't have a job history. What I do have is this, ① G.U.D. certificate, ② Freshman status in the University of the District of Columbia, ③ Certificates for Basic Training in the field of Building Trades.

THE LETTERS IN A RELATIONAL VIEW

The collective story expressed in these letters is dominated by a feeling of dependence. The letter writers are all incarcerated. As such they have severely restricted and controlled freedom. This is the primary punishment of incarceration. But there is more.

The inmates are almost totally dependent on those outside the prison system for assistance in making the transition from cell to society. One person wrote:

> Soon I will be released on parole. My time incarcerated has left me entirely indigient (losing all my worldly possessions) homeless, and jobless. If there is anything at all you could do for me in either of these areas I would be deeply grateful. At present I am merely seeking to pull myself up out of the hole I foolishly dug for myself.

Most of the time, however, the persons they know on the outside don't have many resources and almost certainly no jobs. One person wrote, typically:

> My primary reason for writing your program is to see if I meet the criteria for clothing assistance upon my release. I'll be residing with my mother who is on public assistance, & I am being paroled without employment & clothing.

Inmates are forced to depend on anonymous individuals or organizations for help. Most of the time, they know of these resources only by hearsay and their only means of contact is a hand-written letter. Many of the letters LEEO received indicated from the way they were addressed what the writer knew or did not know about the program: "Dear Mr. LEEO," "Mr. and Mrs. Coordinator," "Dear Sister LEE," or simply "To Whom It May Concern."

By comparison with all the ways a person living in society could make contacts, follow leads, check references, use influence, present an image, the men and women in prison are reduced to an almost cruel dependency. And they sense it.

> I'am also an unexperienced worker, I've never had job now I'am writing you'll in seeking help for a job training or a job of any kind while I'am in training, see I really need your help because since I've been incarcerated I've hada baby and I desperately need a job plus a training so I'am asking for some help of any kind.

They sense their dependency in the lack of response to their meager efforts as well. The silence from the outside is depressing and the depression shows in the letters LEEO received.

> Now I have to do everything on my on because the C & P officer I have now isn't like Mr. C. her name is miss N. and everytime i call up to her office she never want to see me. because she have to many other clients once you made parole and everything they just forget about you. will you please help me I hope I will get a letter back from you by the end of this week.

Every letter LEEO received was answered. Even if the answer was not what the inmate had hoped for, it was an answer, a reply, a communication. That in itself offset a little the feeling of utter dependence on nameless and unresponding sources.

The inmates expressed their sense of dependence in another way. When they did receive a reply (even a form letter) or some other acknowledgment of their request for assistance, they expressed excessive appreciation. One "P.S." stated:

> Thank you for the time in which it has taken you to acknowledge my concerns of my future. I appreciate it from my heart if you could give me some kind of response from my letter in the very near future.

It was not so much that they were being dishonest or manipulative in their gratitude. It was rather that they knew how dependent they were on anyone who would help. A person with many resources and options does not feel the need to be grateful to everyone who is helpful. A person with no assured resources and few options cannot afford not to be grateful to anyone who is helpful. One person indicated the importance of such help by saying:

> In closing, I would like to thank you for your time and for any and all assistance you can provide me. With your response to this letter, I can present it to the parole board and prove to myself as well as others that I can be productive in society, or at least that I am seriously reaching out towards the goal of becoming a living reality in today's society.

Their expression of gratitude was, in most instances, a confirmation of their dependency, but it was also the entry into another set of resources. In fact, it takes very little for an inmate to summon a number of inner, personal strengths to move out of the grasp of dependency and depression. These qualities, listed above, suggest a spirit of *indepen-*

dence which contrasts sharply with the overall condition of dependence which most of them feel.

They are able, for example, to maintain hope despite very discouraging circumstances. They refuse to succumb to the pressure of remaining dependent. They preserve a glimpse of themselves as independent, self-reliant, productive, and responsible. One person stated it forcefully:

> My future as an upstanding citizen in the community after paying back my debt to society depends strongly on me establishing a firm character and sound employment recommendation. With the information that you forward me, Im more than positive that I will successfully fulfill my vision of resurrection. A new man rising from the dead leaving all those negative things behind and charting forward to new horizons.

Often they have no actual experience to match this vision and so cannot anticipate realistically what it will require to become independent. But the lure of freedom and the aim of autonomy remain within. Just a little assurance from outside brings it forth.

In a similar way, they manifest a great openness about themselves. They seem to rely on who they actually are and to feel some confidence in themselves. One person wrote:

> I am an individual looking for a positive change for the better. I have built a strong, positive attitude toward myself and other individuals who are living around me. Also, I have develop a set mind also know what I want for myself.

They know their limits and liabilities, and they are willing to let others know them, too, because within that spectrum they can claim who they really are. The same person who wrote the preceding letter also wrote:

> I will be getting out-of-state parole to Washington, D.C., so I can be able to establish a future for myself in a new state. New York City is a fast growing city and I will be unable to keep up with it, especially just getting out on parole. I know that I will be getting in trouble one way or other. I have family in Washington, D.C., that just move out there during the time I been incarcerated. Thus, I think it will be a good decision.

Part of who they are includes change. They had changed. They had changed internally, by their own choice. This means they are in charge of their lives, they are feeling a little independence. The changes are mostly attitudinal, based on new values and lessons learned from their experience. They are not yet able to demonstrate these changes behaviorally because they are still incarcerated. To this extent, they remain dependent on others to give them a chance. But they know they have changed; they can feel the difference inside and they long to express it outside.

> I need all the help I can get because I have two son's age 3 years and 1 year. Being here not only has proven to me how much my family needs me, but it also has shown me the kind of people I should not have been with when I was at home.

That's why so many of them express a desire to help others when they get out of prison. On the one hand this is an indication of their own felt need for help, transferred to others; on the other hand it is an authentic expression of their feeling that they have something to give which is worth giving and worth receiving. As one person put it,

> I want to spread what I've learned to other's about using drugs and how drugs can ruin your life. Especialy if you don't get off the merry go round before it's too late. I've learned life as it is, is wonderful. I really feel good about myself, for the first time in my life. I want to help other's reach a natural high as I'm having. I'm like a baby with a new toy.

The key to everything for the inmates is a job. This is the way out of the dependency they now experience and into the independence they hope to experience. Employment is the indispensable means, and they know it. But they also know that they are almost totally dependent on others for employment.

> I'am writing you concerning a very important matter. I was granted parole on May 6th 93 days ago, and the only reason why I'am still here at D.C. jail because my parole officer has informed me that I need a job before I can return to the street's. I do not see how I can find a job sitting here in jail, I'am 28 years old, it's not hard for me to find a job if I was out on the street's.

The struggle between dependence and independence structures the daily experience of those in prison. If these two factors were combined in a relational view of life, they would yield an experience of *interdependence*. Interdependence includes elements of both dependence and independence. Because both are included, the negative aspects of each are reduced and the positive aspects increased.

Interdependence recognizes that everyone is already related to everyone else. Despite a heavy emphasis on individualism in American society, the basic and irrefutable fact of life in a relational view is that each person is part of an organic social system. The system is very elastic and admits of a great range of individual autonomy, but it is ultimately limited. The key to its vitality (and to the quality of life within it) is to foster the maximum degree of individual autonomy within an orderly structure that maintains the common good.

This is a great challenge for any social grouping (like a family, a neighborhood, a school, a business, etc.) but it is a staggering challenge for a nation—and for nations as a global society. Nonetheless, if interdependence is claimed as both a value and a goal to be realized in every social grouping, then the challenge needs to be met and met in terms of each particular social situation.

The number of persons being sentenced grows and the construction of new prisons is on the increase. At the same time, the prison system is plagued by serious overcrowding within existing facilities and a lack of effective training and educational programs to prepare persons for the world of work and their transition from the institution to society. There is clearly a disproportionate emphasis. Society seems to do all it can to "put people away" without considering the implications. Most will return. And unless their time of incarceration fosters opportunities for positive behavioral change, the cycle of crime, courts, and convictions will be reenacted.

In view of this, what would it take to enact the goal of interdependence? What steps could be taken to overcome the debilitating dependency of the prison experience and to temper the unrealistic aspirations of the inmates for independence?

Drawing upon the LEEO experience, it is clear that those who now function freely in society, who experience and express their independence, are the ones to make the initial move. Those in prison are in fact dependent but hopefully independent; those in society are in fact independent and hopefully won't become dependent. So, the prospects for interdependence rest on the willingness of people to make the transition from society to the cell.

It is not the purpose of this section to outline a comprehensive rehabilitation program but rather to recommend three areas of service which would improve the quality of life in prison and better prepare persons for their release into society. These are (1) job readiness training, the effective preparation of persons who lack educational and employment qualifications for the world of work; (2) prison industry, the opportunity for job-ready persons to receive job training and/or employment while incarcerated; (3) a network of job-related support services, the provision of postprison assistance for those who maintain employment begun within the institution through prison industry or for those who secure jobs after release.

Job Readiness Training

After having worked with over 1,500 ex-felons, it has been the experience of LEEO that most of these individuals want to be employed and by means of this employment become self-reliant, contributing members of society. However, there is a serious discrepancy between their expressed desire for employment and their actual readiness for the world of work. Seven out of ten LEEO participants were unfamiliar with and unprepared for the responsibilities expected from a job-ready employee. The hours of idleness in prison could be transformed into productive occasions for fostering a prisoner's orientation to and preparation for the world of work. Thousands of imprisoned persons lack work experience and are underemployed. For them, training in work habits, including attitudinal change, is imperative for their adjustment on a job.

Prison Industry

In a speech to the Lincoln Bar Association at the University of Nebraska in December 1981, Chief Justice Warren E. Burger posed the challenge that America's prisons become "factories with fences around them" rather than warehouses. This concept was further explored during a national conference held at George Washington University in Washington, D.C., on June 18, 1984. The theme of the conference was "Factories with Fences: The Prison Industries Approach to Correctional Dilemmas." The Chief Justice emphasized the following:

> The key to every good system I have ever seen is work, education and training. . . . It is on this score that so many of our prisons in this country have been, and are today, an appalling failure for a civilized people.

If the presence of industry in prisons is to be effective, inmates must be able to produce goods for sale outside the institution. Such sales are currently banned by federal law. Retired Chief Justice Burger encourages a change in legislation that would lift "the walls of economic protectionism" which limit the sale of prison goods beyond the state where such goods have been produced.

As of July 1987 there are fifteen projects in which prison inmates are producing goods that are allowed to be placed in interstate commerce or sold to federal agencies. The jurisdictions are: Corrections Departments of Idaho, Kansas, Minnesota, Nevada, New Hampshire's Strafford County, New Mexico, Utah, and Washington; and the California Youth Authority.

The presence of industry within the prison would serve to motivate those who require initial job readiness. Once qualified, they would be included in the industry program. In addition, inmates who are oriented to and prepared for employment would receive skills training as well as develop a work history while participating in the prison industry program. It may be assumed that those who maintain a high level of employability within the prison would be maintained by the industry once they were released.

Network of Job-Related Support Services

In the experience of LEEO, if persons released from prison are to avoid new criminal involvement and are to maintain steady employment, a network of support services must be available to them for at least eight to twelve months following job placement. The particular status of a job and the salary it offers are not enough to assure stabilization of the individual, either on the job or personally. Support will be necessary and must be available. The needs for support which may arise include transportation to and from the work site, uniform or tools required by the job, counseling in conflict situations which may arise between the employee and co-workers or employee and supervisor. Beyond meeting all these needs, the primary service may simply be that the person realizes that someone cares how things are going in this period of transition.

The hundreds of LEEO participants and those who have written for program services are a testimony to the need for employment and job-related assistance. These are specific ways that interdependence could be fostered and society could extend its resources to the cell. Whether these suggestions are followed or not, an appropriate, responsible course of action in this area is urgently needed—not just on the part of the corrections system but also on the part of the society in which these individuals are meant to share life.

THE LETTERS IN A CHRISTIAN VIEW

The letters LEEO received tell again the story of grace. Grace characterizes the relationship between God and human creatures. In that relationship human persons feel themselves to be dependent while God appears to be independent. But in the Jewish and Christian experience, God does not remain independent. Rather, God initiates a relationship, the covenant, whereby people are able to share in God's life while God shares in theirs. This is the primary example of grace in a faith perspective.

The result is a condition of interdependence which can serve as a model for human interaction. Taking the lead from God's example, interdependence occurs when those with resources (experiencing independence) initiate a relationship with those who do not have sufficient resources (experiencing dependence) so that everyone may share in the benefits of the relationship more fully. There are two major challenges to be faced, however.

The first is to get those with resources to initiate a relationship of interdependence. The desire to remain independent and possessive of the means for preserving one's independence is one of the most powerful human experiences. It is not easily altered. In fact, the human history recounted in the Jewish and Christian Scriptures is, in one sense, the story of this struggle. Even God has had an extremely difficult time convincing people that they are all better off if they are interdependent rather than some being independent and others being dependent.

The second challenge is to prevent a new dependency from occurring. Sometimes this can happen without people even knowing it, although most of the time people predetermine how far they will go toward liberating those on the dependency side of the relationship. God has shown a willingness to go as far as it takes, but human persons apply that lesson selectively to themselves.

The perspective of grace offers one other point. The benefits of interdependence are not distributed according to merit or longevity or rank or any other human criterion. Like all grace, they are abundantly given to all who participate. This is the ultimate purpose of initiating such a relationship in the first place. If human effort is truly inspired by God's own gracious movement in human lives (however that movement may be acknowledged or named), then God's grace co-constitutes human effort and the creation of an interdependent relationship in human society will be a reenactment and continuation of God's covenant.

All this may be symbolically expressed in reference to the story Jesus once told about the laborers in the vineyard (Matt. 20:1-16). Jesus likened the reign of God to an owner who had a great vineyard (independence) but needed workers to pick the fruit (dependence). He found some men without work (dependence) and hired them (independence).

But he needed more. So he hired additional workers at midmorning, noon, and midafternoon. Finally, near the end of the day, "he found still others standing around. To these he said, 'Why have you been standing here idle all day?' 'No one has hired us,' they told him. He said, 'You go into the vineyard too.'"

The owner took the initiative to establish a mutually beneficial relationship with all the workers he could find. And to show that the inclusion of all was the primary value, the owner paid the workers all the same wage, beginning with those last hired.

This upset the workers who were first hired and who expected to be paid more. But the owner tried to explain. They had all agreed to work for a certain wage. If it turned out that they all shared equally in the benefits of working together, was that not a blessing for all, a grace, a cause for rejoicing?

Interdependence is a difficult value to affirm in practice, and grace is a demanding gift to accept. But both open the doors to a new relationship between the cell and society. If that relationship is established and if the doors remain open, then society is better cared for. LEEO can attest to that.

Epilogue

W*HEN I RESIGNED* as director of LEEO, I intended to take a short sabbatical and then begin looking for another form of service within the field of corrections. As it turned out, my sabbatical was abbreviated and my next service came looking for me.

Warren E. Burger, then Chief Justice of the U.S., had been promoting the concept of prison reform which he called "factories with fences." Actually, the idea was to expand the existing programs of correctional industries by involving the private sector more extensively.

Chief Justice Burger's hope was that prisoners could be given a realistic work experience while in prison if private sector companies would establish a business operation within the prison, turning correctional facilities in effect into factories with fences around them.

In addition to reducing inmate idleness, this approach could eventually relieve overcrowding if the inmates actually learned a marketable job skill before they were released and used that skill to find employment and not return to crime.

This was a grand vision and it required national support, high visibility, and someone to coordinate the effort. The chief justice was the catalyst. He organized a meeting of top corrections officials, legislators, and media representatives to visit Sweden with him and learn how that country handled their crime problem.

Following this excursion, the Brookings Institute sponsored an invitation-only meeting at the Johnson Foundation Wingspread Conference Center in Racine, Wisconsin, to explore the possibility of taking an innovative prison industry approach to corrections in the U.S.

I was invited to this meeting and to a follow-up conference at George Washington University in June 1984. At this point I was approached by several persons who had been working closely with the chief justice and whom I had come to know as well.

Their plan was to establish a center to foster the chief justice's ideas. The center would be located on the George Washington University campus. They asked me to coordinate its development in cooperation with the dean of continuing education, in whose department the center would be located.

119

My initial responsibility was to coordinate and facilitate another meeting at Wingspread which would formulate recommendations for expanding private sector business in prisons. These recommendations would also be a working agenda for the proposed center.

The center was established in September 1984 with the name National Center for Innovation in Corrections (NCIC). The Second Wingspread Conference was held in February 1985. In May 1985 I was appointed executive director of NCIC. It had not been the sabbatical I anticipated.

The primary goals of NCIC were to be a clearinghouse of information on prison industry programs and to facilitate linkages among interested parties. NCIC was in no position to implement directly any of the fifty recommendations which resulted from the Second Wingspread Conference. (These recommendations have been published under the title *National Conference on Prison Industries: Discussions and Recommendations.*) Neither was NCIC supposed to establish private sector businesses in prisons. Rather, NCIC took a mediating role, identifying interested persons or organizations, facilitating their discussions, and supporting their efforts.

This became a painstaking, slow, and often frustrating process. From September 1984 until September 1987, I identified forty-five potential private sector projects and worked with corrections officials in thirty states. Yet, not one new prison industry resulted. Why?

The primary reason is the complexity of the task, which involves four major components.

First, there is the private sector. After identifying a suitable private sector business, numerous questions have to be resolved such as start-up capital, management of the prison industry, business and labor concerns about the workers and workplace, marketing, and quality control.

Second, there is corrections. Most corrections officials are wary of changes in the prison system, especially if they come from outside the system. Their preoccupation tends to be with maintaining order, and innovation tends to disrupt the status quo.

In addition to this built-in caution, corrections officials would also have to deal with questions about inmate compensation, training of prison personnel to function in a prison industry program, administration of a prison industry within the general prison system, and the selection, training, education, and placement of inmates in jobs.

Third, there is legislation. Generally, prison-made goods cannot be sold in the open market. To make prison industry attractive to the private sector, enabling legislation has to be passed which would allow for sale of goods in public or a corrections department would have to meet the criteria of the Private Sector/Prison Industry Enhancement Certification Program. In either case time-consuming effort is needed before a prison industry can be established.

Fourth, there is public information. Special attempts to help inmates usually meet with resistance from the public at first. After the benefits to society (and the inadequacies of the present system) are pointed out, many people become supportive. I found this to be true especially when I had the opportunity to talk with ordinary citizens on radio call-in shows, TV interviews, or through the editorial page of city newspapers.

The task is complex but not unachievable. In my experience the private sector, legislators, and the public are willing to try a new approach. The major obstacle is corrections.

Officials in the corrections system feel they have too much to lose if prison industry doesn't work well. They also anticipate the problems generated even if it does work well. It simply adds up to too much effort for too little gain.

Of course, without the cooperation of corrections, nothing can happen. On more than one occasion, an entire project was dropped because corrections did not want to go forward with it. It is hard to see how this attitude and power-lock on the system will change soon.

In three years NCIC accomplished what it set out to do. It convened a national meeting on prison industry and published the recommendations from that meeting; it tested the interest of the private sector and found it positive; it acquainted hundreds of people with the legislative changes needed and available; and it helped educate the public at large about current conditions in prisons and the potential of prison industry.

Prison industry remains a viable alternative and a hopeful goal. It is not yet clear how the promise of factories with fences can be realized. But for now, NCIC takes its place with LEEO in the cumulative effort toward the goal of helping inmates make a successful transition from the cell to society.

As a celebration of these years of service, the song on the next page is offered to all those who wish to use it. If there is to be music, we must sing it.

Who Shall Hear?

Lyrics by Bob Kinast
Music by Judith Schloegel
1986

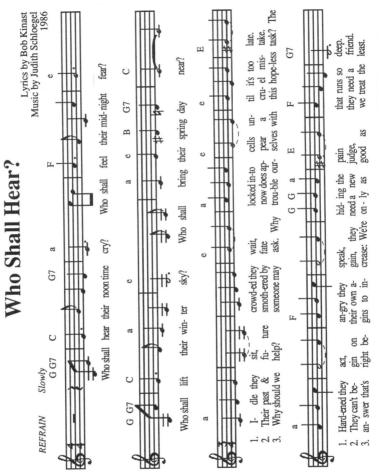

REFRAIN *after each verse*